TENSES ARE MY TEACHER

HINDI TO ENGLISH

PRACTICE PERFECT TENSES

A PRACTICE BOOK

Published on March 17, 2025

AMRITASHAAN

Name & Message

Name

Address

Message

English Speaking

A Practice Book For English Learners

A Practice book

FOR

Present Perfect

Past Perfect

Future Perfect

By : AMRITASHAAN

MY FAMILY

Life is a voyage made possible by the care you give! The entire My Book series pays gratitude to family, and may the spirits be filled with bliss for all.

WELCOME LEARNERS !

It is delightful to see that you are at Vol. 5 and are improving your language proficiency. Through straightforward and highly effective practices, you'll

further gain confidence in your English speaking abilities. Engaging in these exercises will not only familiarize you with the **'has, have, had, will have + 3rd form** of Verb but also enhance your ability to use the correct verbs while conversing in English. Embrace the power of tense as your guide, turning it into your teacher to facilitate effective communication in English.

TABLE OF CONTENTS

TABLE OF CONTENTS

TABLE OF CONTENTS

TABLE OF CONTENTS

TENSES ARE MY TEACHER - Vol. 5
Practice Perfect Tenses

Copyright Office Government Of India
LD-20250166611
Dated : 13/06/ 2025

This self-published book has undergone thorough efforts by the author to ensure the accuracy of its content. Unauthorized usage or reproduction of any part of this book is strictly prohibited without the author's written consent.

The primary goal of this book is to offer learners valuable self-practice material for self-improvement.

Disclaimer: The author has crafted this book based on personal experiences and original ideas. All materials presented are innovative practice resources. It is important to note that this book does not adhere to any prescribed syllabus, although it is highly beneficial for English language learners seeking effective self-practice materials.

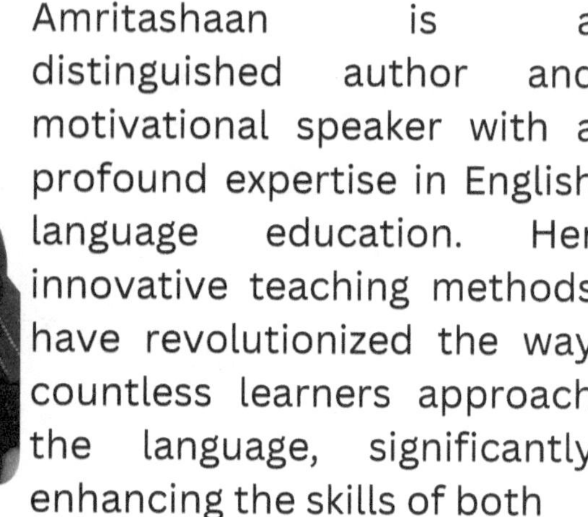

Amritashaan is a distinguished author and motivational speaker with a profound expertise in English language education. Her innovative teaching methods have revolutionized the way countless learners approach the language, significantly enhancing the skills of both native and non-native speakers. With a remarkable collection of books on mastering English, Amritashaan has solidified her reputation as a leading IELTS trainer, making substantial contributions to the field of language education. Her YouTube channel, website serve as a valuable resource, offering insightful guidance and motivation to learners. Whether through her meticulously crafted books or comprehensive practice materials, engaging with her work guarantees an extraordinary and transformative learning experience. In her hometown, she is celebrated as an exceptional educator, admired for her unwavering dedication to the advancement of language teaching.

OBJECTIVE

English has emerged as the primary means of communication for millions of people worldwide. It is employed daily to interact with friends, colleagues, and more. To actively participate in this global discourse, familiarity with English, including a grasp of its various tenses, is essential. The purpose of crafting this book is to:

- Foster a comprehensive understanding of the practical applications of English tenses.
- Facilitate independent practice for learners.
- Supply impactful materials for tangible improvement.
- Enhance proficiency in Hindi-English oral translation for effective English speaking.
- Enable native learners to converse fluently in English.

The fifth volume deals with All Perfect Tenses

PRACTICE WAY

- Tense के नियमों को ध्यान से पढ़ें।
- याद रखें कि आप जिस क्रिया को अभ्यास कर रहे हैं, वह मौलिक क्रिया होनी चाहिए।
- Hindi पाठ को धीरे धीरे पढ़ें।
- धीरे धीरे क्रियाओं को सोचें।
- अब Hindi संस्करण खोलें और पूरे पाठ का अनुवाद करने का प्रयास करें।
- दिए गए क्रियाओं की मदद लें।
- इसे मौखिक रूप से करें।
- अगले पृष्ठ पर अपने काम की जाँच करें।
- नियमित रूप से अभ्यास करें और आत्म विश्वास से बोलें।

- Read the rules of Tense carefully.
- Remember the base verb you are going to practice.
- Read Hindi passage slowly.
- Think of verbs by and by.
- Now keep open Hindi version and try to translate the whole passage in English.
- Take help of given verbs.
- Do it orally.
- Check your work at next page.
- Practice and speak confidently.

Present Perfect Tense (वर्तमान पूर्ण काल) का उपयोग तब किया जाता है जब कोई क्रिया हाल के समय में पूरी हुई हो, या जीवन के अनुभवों, घटनाओं और क्रियाओं को व्यक्त किया जाता है जो वर्तमान समय में प्रभाव डालती हैं।

Present Perfect Tense की संरचना :

1. Subject + has/have + Past Participle (3rd form of verb)
   - Has का प्रयोग I, He, She, It और Singular Subjects के साथ किया जाता है।
   - Have का प्रयोग You, We, They और Plural Subjects के साथ किया जाता है।

उदाहरण:
- मैंने अपना होमवर्क पूरा कर लिया है।
- I have completed my homework.
- उसने अपना काम खत्म कर लिया है।
- She has completed her work.

Rule in HINDI

Present Perfect Tense (Positive) का नियम:

Subject + has/have + past participle (Verb का तीसरा रूप)। यह किसी क्रिया को हाल ही में या वर्तमान में पूरा होने को व्यक्त करता है।

- मैंने अपना होमवर्क पूरा कर लिया है।
- I have finished my homework.
- उसने किताब पढ़ ली है।
- She has read the book.
- वे भारत यात्रा कर चुके हैं।
- They have travelled to India.
- हमने लंच खा लिया है।
- We have eaten lunch.
- वह बाजार गया है।
- He has gone to the market.
- मैंने वह फिल्म देखी है।
- I have seen that movie.
- वह दिल्ली जा चुकी है।
- She has visited Delhi.
- हमने इस प्रोजेक्ट पर काम किया है।
- We have worked on this project.
- उन्होंने मैच जीत लिया है।
- They have won the match.
- आपने अपना काम पूरा कर लिया है।
- You have completed your task.

Present Perfect Tense (Negative) का नियम:

Subject + has/have + not + past participle (Verb का तीसरा रूप)। यह किसी क्रिया को न करने या पूरी न होने को व्यक्त करता है।

Examples:
1. मैंने अपना होमवर्क पूरा नहीं किया है।
2. I have not finished my homework.
3. उसने किताब नहीं पढ़ी है।
4. She has not read the book.
5. वे भारत यात्रा नहीं कर चुके हैं।
6. They have not travelled to India.
7. हमने लंच नहीं खाया है।
8. We have not eaten lunch.
9. वह बाजार नहीं गया है।
10. He has not gone to the market.
11. मैंने वह फिल्म नहीं देखी है।
12. I have not seen that movie.
13. वह दिल्ली नहीं जा चुकी है।
14. She has not visited Delhi.
15. हमने इस प्रोजेक्ट पर काम नहीं किया है।
16. We have not worked on this project.
17. उन्होंने मैच नहीं जीता है।
18. They have not won the match.
19. आपने अपना काम पूरा नहीं किया है।
20. You have not completed your task.

Present Perfect Tense (Interrogative) का नियम:

Has/Have + Subject + Past Participle? यह प्रश्न पूछने के लिए उपयोग किया जाता है कि क्या कोई क्रिया हाल ही में पूरी हुई है या नहीं। Examples:

1.क्या आपने अपना होमवर्कपूरा किया है?

Have you finished your homework?

2. क्या उसने किताब पढ़ी है?

Has she read the book?

3. क्या वे भारत यात्रा कर चुके हैं?

Have they traveled to India?

4. क्या आपने लंच खा लिया है?

Have you eaten lunch?

5. क्या वह बाजार गया है?

Has he gone to the market?

6. क्या आपने वह फिल्म देखी है?

Have you seen that movie?

7. क्या वह दिल्ली गई है?

Has she visited Delhi?

8. क्या आपने इस प्रोजेक्टपर काम किया है?

Have you worked on this project?

9. क्या उन्होंनेमैच जीता है?

Have they won the match?

10. क्या आपने अपना काम पूरा किया है?

Have you completed your task?

Daily Verb Boost

क्रिया	Base Verb	Past Simple	Past Participle
स्वीकार करना	Accept	accepted	accepted
बदलना	Alter	altered	altered
पूछना	Ask	asked	asked
बनाना	Build	built	built
खरीदना	Buy	bought	bought
पकड़ना	Catch	caught	caught
बदलना	Change	changed	changed
साफ करना	Clean	cleaned	cleaned
पकाना	Cook	cooked	cooked
तय करना	Decide	decided	decided
प्रकट करना	Display	displayed	displayed
प्रयास करना	Endeavor	endeavored	endeavored

Daily Verb Boost

क्रिया	Base Verb	Past Simple	Past Participle
नहाना	Bathe	bathed	bathed
झुकना	Bend	bent	bent
तोड़ना	Break	broke	broken
बुलाना	Call	called	called
पकड़ना	Catch	caught	caught
जाँच करना	Check	checked	checked
चुना	Choose	chose	chosen
गिरना	Drop	dropped	dropped
दान देना	Donate	donated	donated
कमाना	Earn	earned	earned
समाप्त करना	End	ended	ended
भरना	Fill	filled	filled

Daily Verb Boost

क्रिया	Base Verb	Past Simple	Past Participle
ढूँढना	Find	found	found
ठीक करना	Fix	fixed	fixed
उड़ना	Fly	flew	flown
भूलना	Forget	forgot	forgotten
माफ करना	Forgive	forgave	forgiven
इकट्ठा करना	Gather	gathered	gathered
प्राप्त करना	Get	got	gotten
देना	Give	gave	given
जाना	Go	went	gone
पकड़ना	Hold	held	held
चोट पहुँचाना	Hurt	hurt	hurt
सुधार करना	Improve	improved	improved

Daily Verb Boost

क्रिया	Base Verb	Past Simple	Past Participle
बढ़ाना	Increase	increased	increased
शोध करना	Investigate	investigated	investigated
शामिल करना	Include	included	included
प्रेरित करना	Inspire	inspired	inspired
स्थापित करना	Install	installed	installed
जाना	Introduce	introduced	introduced
कूदना	Jump	jumped	jumped
जज करना	Judge	judged	judged
जानना	Know	knew	known
रखना	Keep	kept	kept
जान लेना	Learn	learned	learned
छोड़ना	Leave	left	left

Daily Verb Boost

क्रिया	Base Verb	Past Simple	Past Participle
बनाना	Make	made	made
प्रबंधित करना	Manage	managed	managed
मापना	Measure	measured	measured
मिलाना	Meet	met	met
मूर्ख बनाना	Mock	mocked	mocked
घबराना	Panic	panicked	panicked
नया करना	Name	named	named
नोट करना	Note	noted	noted
देखना	Observe	observed	observed
पेश करना	Offer	offered	offered
खोलना	Open	opened	opened
पालन करना	Perform	performed	performed

Daily Verb Boost

क्रिया	Base Verb	Past Simple	Past Participle
प्रतिष्ठित करना	Establish	established	established
बढ़ावा देना	Promote	promoted	promoted
निंदा करना	Denounce	denounced	denounced
संशोधित करना	Modify	modified	modified
प्रकट करना	Reveal	revealed	revealed
आदेश देना	Instruct	instructed	instructed
यथावत रखना	Retain	retained	retained
समेटना	Compile	compiled	compiled
प्रदर्शन करना	Exhibit	exhibited	exhibited
प्रतिस्थापित करना	Substitute	substituted	substituted
पूर्वानुमान करना	Anticipate	anticipated	anticipated

Daily Verb Boost

क्रिया	Base Verb	Past Simple	Past Participle
दौड़ना	Run	ran	run
पढ़ना	Read	read	read
उठाना	Raise	raised	raised
पुनः प्राप्त करना	Recover	recovered	recovered
याद करना	Remember	remembered	remembered
खर्च करना	Spend	spent	spent
रिटायर होना	Retire	retired	retired
बचाना	Save	saved	saved
देखना	See	saw	seen
भेजना	Send	sent	sent
गाना	Sing	sang	sung
बोलना	Speak	spoke	spoken

Daily Verb Boost

क्रिया	Base Verb	Past Simple	Past Participle
उपयोग करना	Use	used	used
समझाना	Understand	understood	understood
उपयोग करना	Utilize	utilized	utilized
विजेता होना	Vanquish	vanquished	vanquished
देखना	View	viewed	viewed
विजेता होना	Verify	verified	verified
विकसीत करना	Vary	varied	varied
जीतना	Win	won	won
इच्छा करना	Wish	wished	wished
लिखना	Write	wrote	written
चेतावनी देना	Warn	warned	warned

Daily Verb Boost

क्रिया	Base Verb	Past Simple	Past Participle
माफी माँगना	Apologize	Apologized	Apologized
आकर्षित करना	Attract	Attracted	Attracted
बाधित करना	Block	Blocked	Blocked
समेटना	Collate	Collated	Collated
भटकाना	Distract	Distracted	Distracted
समाप्त करना	Eliminate	Eliminated	Eliminated
रोकना	Forbid	Forbade	Forbidden
पुनः निर्माण करना	Rebuild	Rebuilt	Rebuilt
विस्तार करना	Lengthen	Lengthened	Lengthened
मॉनिटर करना	Monitor	Monitored	Monitored
उपेक्षा करना	Neglect	Neglected	Neglected

Daily Verb Boost

क्रिया	Base Verb	Past Simple	Past Participle
ग्रहण करना	Assimilate	Assimilated	Assimilated
ज़ब्त करना	Confiscate	Confiscated	Confiscated
विस्तार से समझाना	Elaborate	Elaborated	Elaborated
सुविधा प्रदान करना	Facilitate	Facilitated	Facilitated
सौदेबाजी करना	Negotiate	Negotiated	Negotiated
प्रमाणित करना	Substantiate	Substantiated	Substantiated
स्वतंत्र करना	Emancipate	Emancipated	Emancipated
बढ़ा-चढ़ाकर कहना	Exaggerate	Exaggerated	Exaggerated
घुसपैठ करना	Infiltrate	Infiltrated	Infiltrated
दोषमुक्त करना	Exonerate	Exonerated	Exonerated

Daily Verb Boost

क्रिया	Base Verb	Past Simple	Past Participle
घटाना (डिक्री)	Decrease	Decreased	Decreased
प्रसार करना	Expand	Expanded	Expanded
अनदेखा करना	Ignore	Ignored	Ignored
कल्पना करना	Fantasize	Fantasized	Fantasized
कानूनी बनाना	Legalize	Legalized	Legalized
मार डालना	Kill	Killed	Killed
बाधा डालना	Obstruct	Obstructed	Obstructed
कल्पना करना	Predict	Predicted	Predicted
पुनर्जीवित करना	Revive	Revived	Revived
अलग करना	Segregate	Segregated	Segregated

मैं जॉय हूँ, सात साल का बच्चा हूँ और मैं यहाँ आपकी मदद के लिए हूँ ताकि आप अंग्रेजी बोलने

का अभ्यास कर सकें। मैंने सरल हिंदी में कुछ कहा है, शायद अपने बारे में या किसी अन्य विषय पर। आपका काम है इसे अंग्रेजी में बोलने की कोशिश करना। आपको पूरा अनुवाद धीरे-धीरे मिलेगा, लेकिन उसे देखने से पहले, ईमानदारी से अनुवाद करने और ज़ोर से बोलने का अभ्यास करें।

आपका ईमानदार प्रयास आपको सफलता दिलाएगा और आपकी सफलता आपके दिल को खुशी से भर देगी और आपके मनोबल को ऊंचा उठाएगी!

I'm Joy, a seven-year-old kid and I'm here to help you practice speaking English. I've said something in simple

Hindi—maybe about myself or on different topics. Your job is to try to say it in English. You'll get the full translations  eventually but before you check them, make sure to practice translating and speaking out loud with focus and sincerity.

Your sincere effort will bring you success and your success will fill your heart with joy and uplift your spirit!

Practice Time 1

- जॉय ने अपना काम पूरा कर लिया है और वह सोने चला गया है। (**has completed, has gone**)
- सूरज बादलों के पीछे छिप गया है और अँधेरा हो गया है। (**has hidden, has got**)
- मैंने अंग्रेजी में एक कहानी लिखी है क्योंकि मेरे शिक्षक ने मुझे अंग्रेजी लिखने का अभ्यास करने के लिए कहा है। (**has written, has asked**)
- बच्चे ने सारी सीमाएं लांघ दी हैं और अपने अशिष्ट व्यवहार से उसने अपने माता-पिता को ठेस पहुंचाई है। (**has crossed, has hurt**)
- आपने मेरे सभी संदेह दूर कर दिए हैं और अब मेरे लिए निर्णय लेना आसान हो गया है। (**have cleared, has gone**)
- प्रबंधन ने श्रमिकों की मांग स्वीकार कर ली है और श्रमिक हड़ताल से हट गए हैं। (**has accepted, have taken off**)
- तुमने सच कहा है लेकिन इससे मेरा दिल टूट गया है। (**have spoken, has broken**)
- उनकी महान सफलता ने विश्व को चकित कर दिया है और सभी ने निरन्तर प्रयासों के महत्व को स्वीकार किया है। (**has astonished, has accepted**)

- Joy **has completed** his work and he **has gone** to sleep.
- The sun **has hidden** itself behind the clouds and it **has got** dark.
- I **have written** a story in English because my teacher **has asked** me to practice writing English.
- The child **has crossed** the limits and he **has hurt** his parents with his rude behaviour.
- You **have cleared** my all the doubts and taking decision **has now gone** easy for me.
- The management **has accepted** the demand of the workers and the workers **have taken off** the strike.
- You **have spoken** the truth but it **has broken** my heart.
- His great success **has astonished** the world and everyone **has accepted** the importance of consistent efforts.

- मैंने अभी तक अपना होमवर्क पूरा नहीं किया है और न ही मेरी बहन ने। **(have not completed)**
- उन्होंने कमरा साफ नहीं किया है और बर्तन भी अभी भी गंदे हैं। **(have not cleaned)**
- हमने फिल्म नहीं देखी है और हमें इसकी कहानी भी नहीं पता है। **(have not seen)**
- ट्रेन अभी तक नहीं आई है और बस भी देर से है। **(has not arrived)**
- मैं पेरिस नहीं गया है और मैं लंदन भी नहीं गया हूं। **(have not visited)**
- उसने खाना बनाना शुरू नहीं किया है और टेबल अभी तक सेट नहीं हुई है।**(has not started cooking)**
- उसने अपने माता-पिता को फोन नहीं किया है, और उसने उन्हें ईमेल भी नहीं किया है। **(has not called)**
- प्रबंधक को कोई समाधान नहीं मिला है, और समस्या का समाधान नहीं हुआ है। **(has not found)**
- बच्चों ने अपना होमवर्क नहीं किया है और उन्होंने परीक्षा के लिए पढ़ाई भी नहीं की है। **(have not done)**

- I **have not completed** my homework yet and neither has my sister.
- They **have not cleaned** the room and the dishes are still dirty too.
- We **have not seen** the movie and we don't know the story either.
- The train **has not arrived** yet and the bus is late as well.
- I **have not visited** Paris and I have not been to London either.
- She **has not started** cooking and the table hasn't been set yet.
- He **has not called** his parents and he hasn't emailed them either.
- The manager **has not found** a solution and the problem hasn't been resolved.
- The kids **have not done** their homework and they haven't studied for the test.

- क्या आपने अपना होमवर्क पूरा कर लिया है या आप इसके बारे में भूल गए हैं? (**Have finished**)
- क्या उसने आज आपको फ़ोन किया है या उसने आपको कोई संदेश भेजा है? (**Has called**)
- क्या उन्होंने टिकट बुक कर लिए हैं, या उन्होंने अपनी यात्रा रद्द कर दी है? (**Have booked**)
- क्या हम इस व्यक्ति से पहले मिल चुके हैं या क्या मैंने गलती से उन्हें कोई और समझ लिया है? (**Have met**)
- क्या आपने कभी सुशी आज़माई है या आपने इसे पूरी तरह से त्याग दिया है? (**Have tried**)
- क्या उसने आपको स्थिति समझा दी है या उसने इसे गुप्त रखा है? (**Has explained**)
- क्या आपने संग्रहालय का दौरा किया है या आप इसके बजाय पार्क में गए हैं? (**Have visited**)
- क्या मैंने दरवाज़ा बंद कर दिया है या गलती से खुला छोड़ दिया है? (**Have locked**)
- क्या हमने ईमेल भेजा है या हम इसके बारे में भूल गए हैं? (**Have sent**)
- क्या विद्यार्थियों ने अपना कार्य पूरा कर लिया है या क्या उन्होंने समय सीमा छोड़ दी है? (**Have completed**)

- **Have you finished** your homework or have you forgotten about it?
- **Has she called** you today or has she sent you a message instead?
- **Have they booked** the tickets or have they cancelled their trip?
- **Have we met** this person before or have I mistaken them for someone else?
- **Have you ever tried** sushi or have you avoided it completely?
- **Has he explained** the situation to you or has he kept it a secret?
- **Have you visited** the museum or have you gone to the park instead?
- **Have I locked** the door or have I left it open by mistake?
- **Have we sent** the email or have we forgotten about it?
- **Have the students completed** their assignments or have they skipped the deadline?

- Present Perfect
- Make use of 'Has / Have + 3rd form of verb'
- Negative sentences take 'Has / Have not + 3rd form of verb'
- Interrogative sentences take 'Has / Have + Subject + 3rd form of verb + object?'

The present perfect tense is used to describe actions or events that:

1. Started in the past but have relevance or impact on the present.
2. Occurred recently without specifying an exact time.
3. Happened repeatedly over a period of time up to now.

जॉय का आज फुटबॉल मैच है। उन्होंने अपने खेल आयोजन के लिए कड़ी मेहनत की है। उन्होंने हर दिन अभ्यास किया है और अपने कौशल में सुधार किया है। उन्होंने फिट रहने के लिए एक्सरसाइज की है और हेल्दी खाना खाया है । उन्होंने अपने कोच से भी बात की है, अपने विरोधियों के बारे में जाना है और इवेंट के लिए तैयार होने के लिए अच्छा आराम किया है।

VERBS TO HELP
has, worked, practised, improved, done,
eaten, talked, learned, rested

Joy has his football match today. He has worked hard for his sports event. He has practiced every day and has improved his skills. He

has done exercises to stay fit and has eaten healthy food. He has also talked to his coach, learned about his opponents, and he has recharged his batteries to be ready for the event.

What three important things you have done today?

मेरी माँ का आज जन्मदिन है । मैंने उनके लिए एक विशेष आश्चर्य की व्यवस्था की है। मैंने उनके पसंदीदा फूल और एक सुंदर केक

खरीदा है। मैंने घर पर एक छोटा सा पारिवारिक समारोह आयोजित करने की भी योजना बनाई है। सभी ने अपनी उपस्थिति की पुष्टि कर दी है और मैंने लिविंग रूम को गुब्बारों और उनकी तस्वीरों से सजाया है। मेरी मां को आज अपने जन्मदिन के बारे में भी कोई जानकारी नहीं है।

has, arranged, bought, planned, confirmed, decorated, has no idea - completely in the dark

My mother has her birthday today. I have arranged a special surprise for her. I have bought her favorite flowers and a beautiful cake. I have also planned a small family gathering at home. Everyone has confirmed their attendance and I have decorated the living room with balloons and her photos. My mother is completely in the dark about her birthday today.

What five things have you done to surprise your parents?

GET SET GO

चलिए अब प्रैक्टिस
के लिए
तैयार हो जाइये।

आपको आगे दिए गए सभी पैराग्राफ़ को एक-एक करके पहले हिंदी में पढ़ना है और साथ में उसे मौखिक रूप से इंग्लिश में बोलने की कोशिश करनी है। क्योंकि सभी पैराग्राफ़ का basic Tense, Present Perfect ही है, लेकिन जैसा कि आपने पिछले volumes में Present और Past के अन्य Tense सीख लिए हैं, तो आगे जैसे-जैसे आप 'इंग्लिश बोलो' exercise करेंगे, उनमें मिश्रित टेन्स भी हो सकते हैं। प्रैक्टिस करते-करते आप इस टेन्स को बेहतर ढंग से समझ पाएंगे और आसानी से बोल पाएंगे। प्रतिदिन एक अध्याय का अभ्यास करें और इस पुस्तक को एक महीने में पूरा करें।

जॉय आज पहली बार स्कूल गया है और उसके माता-पिता ने उसे डिवाइन पब्लिक स्कूल में भर्ती करा दिया है। उन्होंने उसके उज्ज्वल भविष्य को सुनिश्चित करने के लिए अपना सर्वश्रेष्ठ प्रयास किया है। जॉय ने बहुत उत्साह के साथ अपना बैग पैक किया है और पूरी सुबह वह बहुत खुश रहा है। उसके माता-पिता ने पहले से ही उसे प्रतिदिन प्रोत्साहित करने की योजना बना ली है ताकि वह जीवन के इस नए अध्याय को जल्दी से अपना सके।

Gone, admitted, put, packed, has been, planned, adapts

Joy has taken his first steps into the world of learning, and his parents have admitted him to Divine Public School.

They have put their best foot forward to ensure his bright future. Joy has packed his bag with great excitement and has been as happy as a lark all morning. His parents have already planned to encourage him daily so that he adapts quickly to this new chapter of life.

Make Sentences

Best foot forward, Bright future,
Happy as a lark, New chapter of life

मैंने हाल ही में साइकिल चलाना सीखा है और यह मेरे लिए बहुत बड़ा बदलाव साबित हुआ है। मेरे माता-पिता ने मुझे मेरे 10वें जन्मदिन पर एक

खूबसूरत साइकिल दी है और तब से मैं बहुत खुश हूँ। इस उपहार ने मेरे जीवन में सकारात्मक बदलाव लाया है। मैं रोजाना साइकिल चलाकर एक नया जीवन जी रहा हूँ, जिससे मेरा स्वास्थ्य बेहतर हुआ है। अब मैं स्कूल बस का इंतजार करने के बजाय साइकिल से स्कूल जाता हूँ। इससे मेरा समय बचता है और मैं खुद को अधिक स्वतंत्र महसूस करता हूँ।

learnt, has been, given, have been, brought, turned over, improved, cycle, saves, makes me feel

I have learnt how to ride a cycle recently, and it has been a game-changer for me. My parents have given me a beautiful cycle on my 10th birthday, and I have been over the moon ever since. This gift has brought a positive change in my life. I have turned over a new leaf by cycling daily, which has improved my health. Now I cycle to school instead of waiting for the school bus. It saves my time and makes me feel more independent.

Make Sentences

A game changer, over the moon, positive change, turn over a new leaf, instead of

मैंने इस साल कई उपलब्धियाँ हासिल की हैं और दुनिया में शीर्ष पर महसूस किया है। मेरी टीम ने

मेरे साथ मिलकर काम किया है और साथ मिलकर हमने कठिन चुनौतियों का सामना किया है। हमने अपने प्रयासों के लिए पहचान अर्जित की है, जो कि सोने पर सुहागा है। इन उपलब्धियों ने हमारा आत्मविश्वास बढ़ाया है और हमें दिखाया है कि कड़ी मेहनत हमेशा अंत में रंग लाती है।

Achieved, felt, worked, tackled, earned, has been, boosted, shown, pays off

Speak English - 3

I have achieved many milestones this year and have felt on top of the world. My team has worked hand in hand with me and

together, we have tackled tough challenges. We have earned recognition for our efforts which has been the icing on the cake. These accomplishments have boosted our confidence and shown us that hard work always pays off in the end.

Make Sentences

Achieve milestones, on top of the world, hand in hand, earn recognition, accomplishments

जॉय ने आज एक पक्षी की मदद की है और उसे बचाया है जिस पर गली की एक बिल्ली ने हमला किया था। उसने

गौरैया को मुसीबत में देखते ही तुरंत कार्रवाई शुरू कर दी है। उसे बचाने के लिए उसने जोर से ताली बजाई है और चिल्लाया, जिससे बिल्ली डरकर भाग गई है। उसने डरी हुई चिड़िया को धीरे से उठाकर सुरक्षित स्थान पर रखकर एक और अच्छा काम किया है। उसकी समझदारी और समय पर की गई कार्रवाई वास्तव में उस छोटी चिड़िया के लिए वरदान साबित हुई है।

helped, saved, was attacked, jumped, saw, clapped, shouted, scared, gone, proved

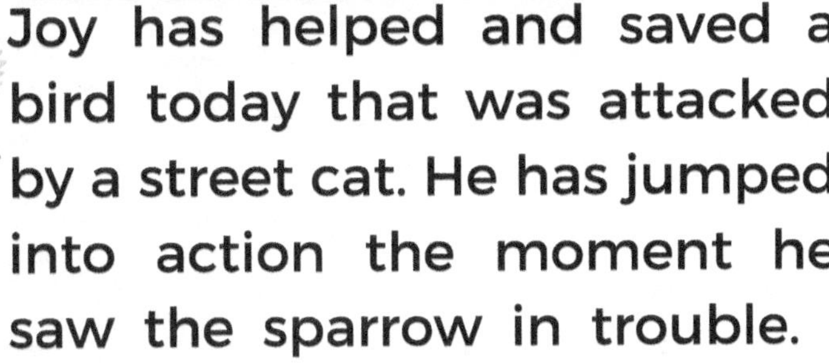

Joy has helped and saved a bird today that was attacked by a street cat. He has jumped into action the moment he saw the sparrow in trouble.

To save it, he has clapped his hands loudly and shouted, which has scared the cat away. He has gone the extra

mile by gently picking up the frightened bird and placing it in a safe spot. His wisdom and timely action has truly proved a blessing in disguise for the little bird.

Make Sentences

Jump into action, scare away, to go extra mile, blessing in disguise

जॉय ने एक बुद्धिमान राजा और उसके साहसी निर्णयों के बारे में एक अद्भुत कहानी पढ़ी है। कहानी में, राजकुमार ने एक बाघ का पिंजरा खोल दिया है, जिससे बहुत बड़ा खतरा पैदा हो गया है। समस्या को ठीक करने के लिए, उसने जॉय को बाघ को वापस पिंजरे में डालने का आदेश दिया है। जॉय ने राजा के न्याय के द्वार पर दस्तक दी है। राजा ने राजकुमार को उसकी मूर्खता के लिए जेल भेजकर न्याय किया है। इस कहानी ने जॉय को एक सबक सिखाया है, हमें कार्य करने से पहले सोचना चाहिए।

read, opened, ordered, knocked, done, taught, think

Speak English - 5

Joy has read an amazing story about a wise king and his brave decisions. In the story, the prince has opened the cage of a tiger, causing great danger. To fix the problem, he has ordered Joy to put the tiger back in the cage. Joy has knocked at the king's justice door. The king has done justice by sending the prince to jail for his foolishness.

This story has taught Joy a lesson that we must think before we act.

Make Sentences

Amazing story, brave decision, to fix the problem, knock at the door of justice

मैंने अपने अंग्रेजी बोलने के कौशल को सुधारने में महत्वपूर्ण प्रगति की है। जैसा कि कहावत है, "अभ्यास मनुष्य को पूर्ण बनाता है," मैंने इसे प्राप्त करने के लिए लगन से अभ्यास किया है। सबसे पहले, मैंने टेन्सेस आर माई टीचर पुस्तक का उपयोग करके काल पर महारत हासिल करने पर ध्यान केंद्रित किया है। इसके अतिरिक्त, मैंने एक विशेषज्ञ अंग्रेजी प्रशिक्षक के मार्गदर्शन में अभ्यास किया है, जिन्होंने मुझे स्पष्ट दिशा और आत्मविश्वास दिया है। अपनी शब्दावली का विस्तार करने के लिए, मैंने अच्छी किताबें पढ़ी हैं और नए शब्द सीखे हैं। इसके अलावा, मैंने अपने आराम क्षेत्र से बाहर निकलकर उन लोगों के साथ अंग्रेजी बोलने की कोशिश की है जो धाराप्रवाह हैं। इससे मुझे स्वाभाविक बातचीत के गुर सीखने में मदद मिली है। ये सभी प्रयास वास्तव में सफल हुए हैं और दिखाया है कि "सफलता उन्हीं को मिलती है जो इसके लिए काम करते हैं।"

made, says, makes, practised, focused, given, read, learned, stepped out, helped, borne fruit

Speak English - 6

I have made significant progress in improving my English-speaking skills. As the proverb says, "Practice makes a man perfect," I have practised diligently to achieve this. First, I have focused on mastering tenses by using the book Tenses Are My Teacher. Additionally, I have practised under the guidance of an expert English trainer who has given me clear direction and confidence. To expand my vocabulary, I have read good books and learned new words. Moreover, I have stepped out of my comfort zone and tried speaking English with people who are fluent. This has helped me learn the ropes of natural conversation. All these efforts have truly borne fruit and shown that "Success comes to those who work for it."

जॉय घर का रास्ता भूल गया है! उसने अपनी क्लास जल्दी छोड़ दी है और चुपके से स्कूल से बाहर निकल गया है।

लगता है कि उसने अपनी क्षमता से ज्यादा काम करने की कोशिश की है, क्योंकि अब उसे सड़कें बिल्कुल अनजान लग रही हैं। जॉय याद करने की उम्मीद में चक्कर काट रहा है, लेकिन किस्मत ने अभी तक उसका साथ नहीं दिया है। यह अप्रत्याशित घटना उसे सच में एक मुश्किल स्थिति में डाल चुकी है—क्या मुसीबत में फंस गया है!

has forgotten, left, sneak out, seems, bitten off, look, has been running, smiled

Joy has forgotten the way home! He has left his class early, sneaking out of school under the radar. It seems he has bitten off more than he can chew, as the

streets now look completely unfamiliar. Joy has been running in circles, hoping to jog his memory, but luck hasn't smiled on him yet. This unexpected adventure has surely put him between a rock and a hard place—what a pickle he's in!

UNDERSTAND THE USE OF IDIOMS
sneak out of, bite off than one can chew, jog one's memory, between rock and hard place, a pickle one is in

जॉय ने झूठ बोला है, दावा किया है कि उसे पेट दर्द हो रहा है ताकि वह अपने दोस्तों के साथ खेलने से

बच सके। उसे क्या पता है कि उसका झूठ उल्टा पड़ गया है । इसके परिणामस्वरूप, वह जादू शो का टिकट जीतने का मौका खो बैठा है।

उसके दोस्त, जो पार्क में एक जादूगर से मिले है , अब उसके जादू शो के मुफ्त टिकट लेकर खुशी से झूम रहे हैं। जॉय को अब देर से एहसास हुआ है कि ईमानदारी सबसे अच्छी नीति है और उसका पछतावा उसे बहुत गहरे तक झकझोर गया है।

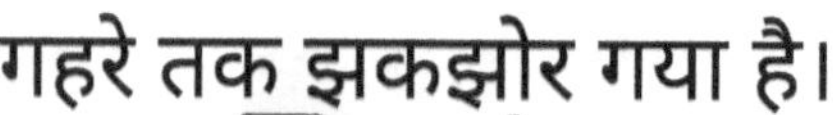

Joy has told a lie, claiming he has a stomachache to skip playing with his friends. Little does he know, his fib has backfired! As a

result, he has missed the boat to win a ticket to the magic show. His friends, who have happened to meet a magician in the park are now jumping for joy with their free tickets to his magic show in hand. Joy has realized too late that honesty is the best policy, and his regret has hit him like a ton of bricks.

Fib has backfired, missed the boat, regret has hit him like a ton of bricks

मैंने आज अपनी टीचर से सबसे चौंकाने वाली खबर सुनी है। उन्होंने पूरे स्कूल को बताया है कि हमें अगले महीने राष्ट्रीय विज्ञान प्रदर्शनी की मेज़बानी के लिए चुना

गया है। क्या आप इस पर यकीन कर सकते हैं? यह तो ऐसा है जैसे हमें कोई बड़ा खज़ाना मिल गया हो! उन्होंने यह भी याद दिलाया है कि टीमवर्क से ही सपना सच होता है, इसलिए हर किसी को योगदान देना होगा। आखिर में, उन्होंने वादा किया है कि वह हर कदम पर हमारा मार्गदर्शन करेंगी क्योंकि उन्हें विश्वास है कि हम इसे शानदार तरीके से पूरा कर सकते हैं ।

Speak English - 9

I have just heard the most astonishing news from my teacher today! She has told the whole school that we have been chosen to host the national science exhibition next month. Can you believe it? It is like we have hit the jackpot! She has also reminded us that teamwork makes the dream work, so everyone must contribute.

Lastly, she has promised to guide us every step of the way because she believes we can pull this off with flying colors.

Make Sentences

Hit the jackpot, Pull something off, Flying colors

जॉय थक गया है क्योंकि उसने आज तीन शारीरिक रूप से थकाने वाले काम पूरे किए हैं। सबसे पहले, उसने भारी फर्नीचर को लिविंग रूम में शिफ्ट किया है और आने वाले त्योहार के लिए जगह तैयार की, जिससे उसे

वाकई बहुत मेहनत करनी पड़ी। इसके बाद, उसने पूरे पिछवाड़े की सफाई की है और कोई कसर नहीं छोड़ी। आखिर में, उसने सीढ़ियों पर भारी राशन का सामान उठाकर ले गया, जो उसके लिए आखिरी झटका साबित हुआ। इन कामों ने उसे पूरी तरह थका दिया है, और अब उसे थोड़ा आराम करने की जरूरत महसूस हो रही है। जॉय ने समझ लिया है कि अपनी क्षमता से ज्यादा जिम्मेदारी लेना हमेशा सही नहीं होता ।

> got tired, completed, moved, prepared, cleaned, carried, felt, left, feels the need, realized

Speak English - 10

Joy is tired because he has completed three physically demanding tasks today. First, he has moved heavy furniture to the living room and prepared the ground for the

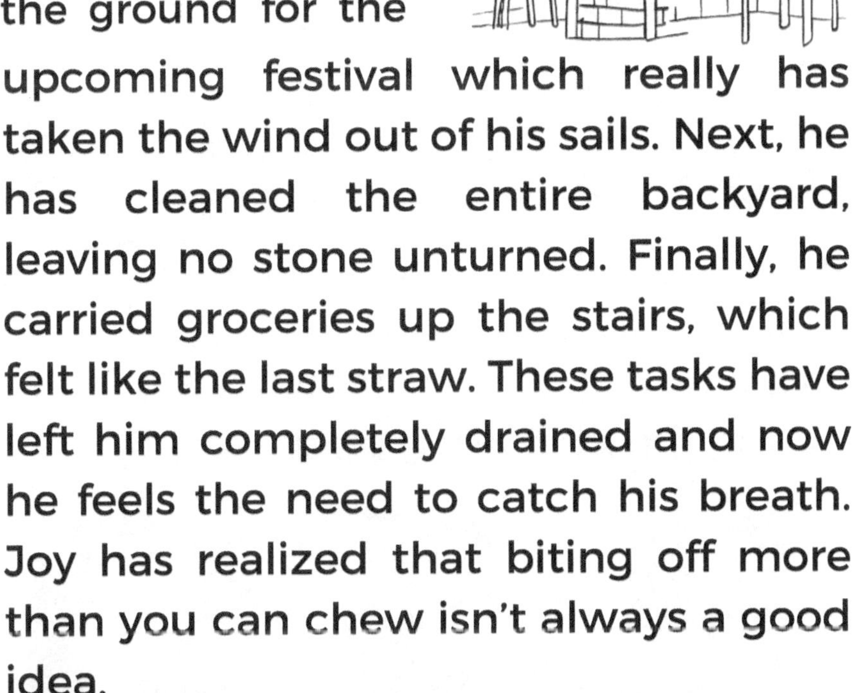

upcoming festival which really has taken the wind out of his sails. Next, he has cleaned the entire backyard, leaving no stone unturned. Finally, he carried groceries up the stairs, which felt like the last straw. These tasks have left him completely drained and now he feels the need to catch his breath. Joy has realized that biting off more than you can chew isn't always a good idea.

MAKE SENTENCES
Feel like the last straw, to catch the breath

विज्ञान ने शिक्षा को अद्भुत तरीकों से बदल दिया है। इसने हमें स्मार्टबोर्ड और ऑनलाइन कक्षाएं दी हैं, जिससे सीखना आसान और मजेदार हो गया है।

अब छात्र अपने उपकरणों पर एक क्लिक से कई चीजें सीख सकते हैं। उन्होंने ऑनलाइन प्रयोग किए हैं और नए विषयों को बेहतर तरीके से समझा है। शिक्षकों ने पाठों को साफ-साफ समझाने के लिए ऐप्स और उपकरणों का इस्तेमाल किया है। विज्ञान ने छात्रों और शिक्षकों को दूर-दूर से एक-दूसरे से बात करने में भी मदद की है। इन बदलावों ने शिक्षा को हर किसी के लिए बेहतर और रोचक बना दिया है।

Science has changed education in amazing ways. It has given us smartboards and online classes, making learning easy and fun. Students can now learn many things with just one click on their devices. They have done experiments online and understood new topics better. Teachers have used apps and tools to explain lessons clearly. Science has also helped students and teachers talk to each other from faraway places. These changes have breathed a new life into education, making it better and more exciting for everyone.

Which change of science do you admire the most?

पैसेंजर पिजन कभी उत्तर अमेरिका में सबसे अधिक संख्या में पाई जाने वाली पक्षी थी, जिसकी अरबों की तादाद वाले झुंड आसमान को भर देते थे।

दुख की बात है कि यह अद्भुत पक्षी अब हमारे पर्यावरण से गायब हो चुका है। यह मानव लालच का शिकार बन गया है। समय के साथ, लोगों ने इसे भोजन और पंखों के लिए बेरहमी से शिकार किया है। व्यापक वनों की कटाई ने इसके घोंसले बनाने के स्थानों को नष्ट कर दिया है। पैसेंजर पिजन ने मानव लापरवाही की भारी कीमत चुकाई है। यह केवल यादें और पछतावा ही छोड़ गया है। इसका विलुप्त होना उस नुकसान का भयावह प्रतीक बन गया है हमने क्या खोया है।

Speak English - 12

The Passenger Pigeon was once one of the most abundant birds in North America, with billions of them filling the skies in  massive flocks. Sadly, this remarkable bird has vanished from our environment. It has become a victim of human exploitation. Over time, people have hunted it relentlessly for food and feathers. The widespread deforestation has destroyed its nesting grounds. The Passenger Pigeon has paid the ultimate price for human carelessness. It has left behind only memories and regret. Its extinction has become a haunting symbol of what we have lost.

कृत्रिम बुद्धिमत्ता (AI) ने अपनी अविश्वसनीय शक्तियों से दुनिया को चकित कर दिया है। इसने हमारे जीने, सीखने और काम करने के तरीके को उन तरीकों से बदल दिया है जिनकी हमने कभी कल्पना भी नहीं की थी। एआई ने कठिन समस्याओं को हल किया है, खूबसूरत चित्र बनाए हैं और यहां तक कि कहानियां भी लिखी हैं। इसने डॉक्टरों को बेहतर इलाज और बीमारियों का जल्दी पता लगाकर जीवन बचाने में मदद की है। लोगों ने ऐसे रोबोट बनाए हैं जो इंसानों की तरह काम करते हैं और चैटबॉट जो दोस्तों की तरह बात करते हैं। सबसे आश्चर्यजनक बात यह है कि एआई ने ऐसे चेहरे बनाए हैं जो इतने असली लगते हैं कि वे लड़के या लड़कियों की तरह दिखते हैं और यह विश्वास करना मुश्किल हो जाता है कि वे इंसान नहीं हैं। वास्तव में, एआई ने हमें भविष्य के चमत्कार दिए हैं और हमें प्रौद्योगिकी का जादू दिखाया है।

has amazed, changed, imagined, solved, painted, written, helped, built, created, brought, shown

Artificial Intelligence has amazed the world with its unbelievable powers. It has changed how we live, learn, and work in ways we had never imagined. AI has solved hard problems, painted beautiful pictures, and even written stories. It has helped doctors save lives by giving better treatment and finding diseases early. People have built robots that act like humans and chatbots that talk like friends. Most amazingly, AI has created faces so real they look like boys or girls, making it hard to believe they are not human. Truly, AI has brought us the wonders of the future and has shown us the magic of technology.

Make a presentation on The Importance of AI

मुंडन संस्कार भारतीय संस्कृति में एक महत्वपूर्ण पारंपरिक समारोह है। जोय ने सीखा कि यह एक रीति है जिसमें नवजात शिशु के जन्म के बाल शेव  किए जाते हैं। परिवारों का मानना है कि यह रीति बच्चे को पिछले जन्म की अशुद्धियों से शुद्ध करती है और उसे एक स्वस्थ और समृद्ध जीवन के लिए आशीर्वाद देती है। एक नाई ने समारोह के दौरान बच्चे के सिर को ध्यान से शेव किया है और दादा-दादी ने बच्चे को एक सोने की चेन देकर आशीर्वाद दिया है। अब बच्चे के सिर के साफ और चमकदार बालों के साथ उसकी एक नई, प्यारी रूप-रचना है। यह समारोह प्रार्थनाओं और उत्सवों के साथ किया गया है, जिससे यह रिश्तेदारों और दोस्तों के लिए एक खुशी का अवसर बन गया है।

has learned, is shaved, believe, cleanses, brings, shaved, blessed, has been performed

Speak English - 14

Tonsure is an important traditional ceremony in Indian culture. Joy has learned that it is a ritual where the  birth hair of a newborn child is shaved. Families believe this ritual cleanses the baby of past birth impurities and brings blessings for a healthy and prosperous life. A barber has carefully shaved the baby's head during the ceremony, and the grandparents have blessed the child by giving a gold chain. The baby boy now has a new, cute look with his shiny, clean head. The ceremony has been performed with prayers and celebrations, making it a joyful occasion for relatives and friends.

Make a presentation on some ritual in your family

कचरे की बढ़ती समस्या हमारे देश में एक महत्वपूर्ण मुद्दा बन चुकी है, जबकि अन्य देश अपनी सफाई और सुंदर परिवेश के लिए प्रसिद्ध हैं। इस समस्या का समाधान करने के

लिए भारतीय सरकार ने स्वच्छ भारत अभियान की शुरुआत की है। इस पहल ने नागरिकों को सफाई बनाए रखने, कचरे का सही तरीके से निपटान करने और सार्वजनिक स्थानों पर कचरा न फैलाने के लिए प्रेरित किया है। सरकार ने देशवासियों से यह भी अपेक्षा की है कि वे सफाई अभियानों में सक्रिय रूप से भाग लें और भारत को एक साफ और आकर्षक राष्ट्र बनाएं।

has become, started, encouraged, expected,

Increasing garbage has become a significant problem in our country, while other nations are renowned for their cleanliness and beautiful surroundings.

To address this, the Indian government has started the Clean India Campaign. This initiative has encouraged citizens to maintain cleanliness, properly dispose of waste, and avoid littering in public places. The government has also expected countrymen to actively participate in cleanliness drives, make India a cleaner and more attractive nation.

Make a presentation The Clean India Campaign

- **Fill in the blanks. Use the present perfect tense.**
  - She ___ **(complete)** her project ___. **(already)**
  - I ___ **(not/finish)** my homework ___. **(yet)**
  - They ___ **(travel)** to Europe ___. **(three times)**
  - He ___ **(work)** at this company ___ 2010. **(since)**
  - We ___ **(visit)** the zoo ___. **(recently)**
  - ___ you ___ **(see)** this movie? **(ever)**
  - My friends ___ **(not/decide)** where to go for dinner ___. **(yet)**
  - I ___ **(never/eat)** sushi before. **(never)**
  - She ___ **(just/arrive)** at the airport. **(just)**
  - ___ they ___ **(read)** the book you recommended? **(yet)**
  - I ___ **(live)** in this city ___ five years. **(for)**
  - He ___ **(always/want)** to learn French. **(always)**
  - We ___ **(not/meet)** him before. **(before)**
  - The baby ___ **(fall)** asleep ___. **(already)**
  You ___ **(finish)** your homework yet?

Check your Answer : -

1. She **has completed** her project already.
2. I **have not finished** my homework yet.
3. They **have travelled** to Europe three times.
4. He **has worked** at this company since 2010.
5. We **have visited** the zoo recently.
6. **Have you seen** this movie ever?
7. My friends **have not decided** where to go for dinner yet.
8. I **have never eaten** sushi before.
9. She **has just arrived** at the airport.
10. **Have they read** the book you recommended yet?
11. I **have lived** in this city for five years.
12. He **has always wanted** to learn French.
13. We **have not met** him before.
14. The baby **has already fallen** asleep.
15. **Have you finished** your homework yet?

Instructions:

Each sentence contains **an error**. Identify the mistake and rewrite the sentence correctly.

1. She has went to the market to buy some groceries.
2. They hasn't finished their homework yet.
3. I am lived in this city for five years.
4. Have you ever eat sushi before?
5. He has just wrote a beautiful poem for the competition.
6. We didn't visited our grandparents this year.
7. She has be here since morning.
8. The children has already gone to the park.
9. I have not saw him at the party yesterday.
10. Have the teacher explained the topic to the students?
11. We has completed the project on time.
12. My friends hasn't arrived at the station yet.
13. She haven't taken any rest since the morning.
14. They have returned the books yesterday.
15. He has been never to Paris before.

Correct Answers:

1. She has **gone** to the market to buy some groceries.
2. They **haven't** finished their homework yet.
3. I have **lived** in this city for five years.
4. Have you ever **eaten** sushi before?
5. He has just **written** a beautiful poem for the competition.
6. We **haven't** visited our grandparents this year.
7. She has **been** here since morning.
8. The children **have** already gone to the park.
9. I have not **seen** him at the party yesterday.
10. **Has** the teacher explained the topic to the students?
11. We **have** completed the project on time.
12. My friends **haven't** arrived at the station yet.
13. She **hasn't** taken any rest since the morning.
14. They **returned** the books yesterday.
(*Use Simple Past for definite past time markers like "yesterday.")
15. He has **never been** to Paris before.

Speaking Practice

Answer Questions for Daily Conversation

- Have you finished your homework?
- Have you had breakfast yet?
- Have you ever been to a zoo?
- Have you called your friend today?
- Have you cleaned your room?
- Have you seen the new movie?
- Have you watered the plants?
- Have you spoken to Mom about the party?
- Have you read this book before?
- Have you visited the doctor recently?
- Have you found your keys?
- Have you sent the email?
- Have you tried this recipe before?
- Have you taken Furry for a walk today?
- Have you met the new neighbor?
- Have you ever traveled by train?
- Have you completed your project?
- Have you talked to Dad about your plan?
- Have you charged your phone?
- Have you ever played this game before?

डॉक्टर: जॉय, लगता है तुमने खाने-पीने की आदतों में लापरवाही बरत कर खुद को मुश्किल में डाल लिया है। क्या तुमने खाने से पहले ठीक से हाथ धोए थे?

जॉय: मैंने पूरी कोशिश की, लेकिन शायद कुछ बार शॉर्टकट ले लिया। क्या इसी वजह से मैं बीमार महसूस कर रहा हूं?

डॉक्टर: बिल्कुल! तुमने सफाई में चूक की और अब कीटाणु तुम्हारे पेट में जश्न मना रहे हैं।

जॉय: ओह नहीं! इस बार मैंने कड़वा सबक सीख लिया है।

डॉक्टर: अच्छा है! साफ हाथ सेहत के लिए सोने के भाव होते हैं। क्या तुमने इसे नियमित रूप से अपनाया है?

जॉय: सच कहूं तो, मैंने कभी-कभार हाथ धोए हैं, लेकिन इसे प्राथमिकता नहीं दी।

डॉक्टर: खैर, अब इसकी कीमत चुका रहे हो। आज से वादा करो कि सफाई को नजरअंदाज करना बंद करोगे।

जॉय: आप सही कह रहे हैं, डॉक्टर! मैंने अब से सुधरने का फैसला कर लिया है—मैंने हर कोने में साबुन रख दिया है!

Enjoying Learning Idioms with Conversation Practice

Doctor: Joy, it seems you've been burning the candle at both ends with your eating habits. Have you washed your hands properly before meals?

Joy: I've tried my best, but maybe I've cut corners a few times. Is that why I'm feeling under the weather?

Doctor: Exactly! You've let germs slip through the cracks, and now they've had a field day in your stomach.

Joy: Oh no! I've learned my lesson the hard way this time.

Doctor: Good! Clean hands are worth their weight in gold when it comes to staying healthy. Have you followed this habit regularly?

Joy: Honestly, I've washed my hands now and then, but I haven't made it a priority.

Doctor: Well, you've paid the price for it now. From today, promise me you'll stop turning a blind eye to hygiene.

Joy: You're right, Doc! I've turned over a new leaf already—I've got soap in every corner of the house now!

Practice Conversation

Teacher: Joy, I have just found out you write poems. Is that true?

Joy: Yes, ma'am, I do, but I haven't shared them with anyone yet.

Teacher: Oh, i see! I have seen one of your poems, and it's wonderful!

Joy: Thank you, ma'am. I've been writing for two years, but I have never thought they were good enough.

Teacher: That's not true! You have great talent. Have you ever thought of getting them published?

Joy: No, I haven't thought of that.

Teacher: Well, now's the time! Write five of your best poems, and I'll make sure they're in the school magazine.

Joy: Really? I've never imagined that! I feel excited about it. I will work on them and share them with you soon.

Teacher: Believe in yourself, Joy. Have you already started working on any new poem?

Joy: Yes, ma'am. I've started one today. I'll include it in the five!

Teacher: All the best !

Brother: Have you eaten the last slice of pizza? I've been hunting high and low for it!

Sister: No, I haven't eaten it... but maybe the dog has. He's been acting like a wolf in sheep's clothing lately.

Brother: Really? Have you taught the dog to pinch food?

Sister: I haven't taught him, but he's picked it up. He's got a taste for the finer things in life—just like you!

Brother: Watch your tongue, or you'll bite off more than you can chew!

Sister: Keep your shirt on! I was only joking.

Brother: Have you seen my headphones? They've vanished into thin air.

Sister: I haven't seen them, but I've borrowed them.

Brother: Borrowed? Have you taken them again? You're skating on thin ice!

Sister: Yes, I've taken them, and I've had the time of my life using them!

Joy: Alex, I want to get a dog but my mother says that keeping a dog is a costly affair.

Alex: Pets do cost money, Joy, but they're amazing companions. Have you talked to your dad?

Joy: Yes, he might agree if I promise to take full responsibility.

Alex: That's fair. I have a dog, and trust me, it's a lot of work—daily walks, feeding, grooming. Are you ready for that?

Joy: I think I am.

Alex: Have you considered adopting instead of buying? It's cheaper and more meaningful.

Joy: I haven't thought about that, but it sounds like a great idea. What breed do you think is good for an apartment?

Alex: Smaller breeds are usually better spaces.

Joy: I'll look into shelters then.

Alex: Smart move.

Joy: Thanks, Alex. I'll work on that. I really hope they agree!

Alex: They will, Joy. Just show them you're serious and responsible. You'll love having a dog!

Jini: "Joy, I am so happy we are getting a dog!"

Joy: "I told you I would convince Mom and Dad. It wasn't that hard!"

Jini: "But I am worried, Joy. You are lazy. Will you take care of the dog?"

Joy: "Of course, I will! I will feed the dog, take it for walks and play with it every day."

Jini: "Really? What if you forget? You always forget things."

Joy: "Not this time, Jini. I promise I will do everything. You too are there to help me!"

Jini: "Please don't rely on me as i'm highly occupied with my studies. But I will watch you. If you don't take care of the dog, I will complain to Mom and Dad."

Joy: "Fine, watch me! Our dog will love me the most!"

Jini: "Let's see, Joy. I hope you are serious this time."

Joy: "Don't worry, Jini. I will prove you wrong!"

Jini: "I'll be happy!

Mother: "Joy, how has your day been with Furry? Have you managed everything well?"

Joy: "It has been great, Mom! I have taken him for two walks and he enjoyed them so much."

Mother: "Really? That's good to hear. Have you fed him on time?"

Joy: "Yes, I have given him his meals exactly as per the schedule. He has finished everything happily."

Mother: "That's impressive, Joy! What about cleaning his space?"

Joy: "Of course, I have! His area is neat, and I even brushed him in the afternoon. He looks so shiny now!"

Mother: "I am proud of you, Joy. You have become so responsible. I can see you are putting real effort into taking care of Furry."

Joy: "Thanks, Mom! Honestly, I feel more active now. Playing with Furry and taking care of him has been fun."

Mother: "I can see that. Keep it up, Joy."

Joy: "Don't worry, Mom. I will keep doing my best. Furry has become my best friend already."

1. What has the farmer done with the crops before the rain starts?
2. Has the farmer repaired the fence before it begins to rain?
3. Where has the farmer stacked the hay bales before the storm arrives?
4. Why has the farmer fed the chickens earlier that day?
5. Which seeds has the farmer planted before the sky turns dark?

1. What innovative features have the students included in their pollution control project?
2. Have they explained how the wind turbines contribute to reducing pollution?
3. How many models of green energy solutions have they created for the project?
4. Have the students showcased the importance of solar panels in their presentation?
5. Who has visited their project booth to learn about their ideas?

Make Your Notes

Make Your Notes

LET'S
GO TO THE NEXT TENSE

PAST PERFECT

UNDERSTAND PAST PERFECT

Past Perfect Tense का उपयोग उन कार्यों या घटनाओं को व्यक्त करने के लिए किया जाता है जो अतीत में किसी अन्य कार्य या समय से पहले पूरी हो चुकी थीं। इसमें यह संकेत मिलता है कि एक क्रिया पहले पूरी हो चुकी है।

इस काल की पहचान "had" सहायक क्रिया और मुख्य क्रिया के तीसरे रूप (Past Participle) का उपयोग करके होती है।

सकारात्मक वाक्य: जिनमें **"लिया था," "गया था," "देखा था," "सुना था," "मिले थे," "भागा था"** जैसे भाव व्यक्त किए जाते हैं।

सर्वनाम + had + क्रिया (तीसरा रूप) + बाकी वाक्य

उदाहरण:

मैंने अपना काम पूरा कर लिया था।

(I had completed my work.)

नकारात्मक वाक्य: सर्वनाम + had + not + क्रिया (तीसरा रूप) + बाकी वाक्य उदाहरण:

हमने उस पुस्तक को नहीं पढ़ा था।

(We had not read that book.)

प्रश्नवाचक वाक्य: Had + सर्वनाम + क्रिया (तीसरा रूप) + बाकी वाक्य?

उदाहरण:

क्या उसने यह खबर सुनी थी?

(Had he heard this news?)

UNDERSTAND PAST PERFECT

Affirmative Sentences:

Subject + had + past participle + rest of the sentence

- I had taken the book.
- He had gone to the market.
- We had watched the movie.
- She had heard the song.
- They had met at the fair.
- The boy had run fast.

Negative Sentences:

Subject + had + not + past participle + rest of the sentence

- I had not taken the book.
- He had not gone to the market.
- We had not watched the movie.
- She had not heard the song.
- They had not met at the fair.
- The boy had not run fast.

Interrogative Sentences:

Had + subject + past participle + rest of the sentence?

- Had you taken the book?
- Had he gone to the market?
- Had we watched the movie?
- Had she heard the song?
- Had they met at the fair?
- Had the boy run fast?

Practice Time 1

- उसने पहले ही निर्णय ले लिया था। **(had taken)**
- मैंने नई गाड़ी खरीदने का निर्णय ले लिया था। **(had decided)**
- उसने अपने दोस्तों को पार्टी के लिए पहले ही बुला लिया था। **(had invited)**
- उन्होंने यह विचार पहले से ही कर लिया था। **(had thought)**
- माँ ने हमारे आने से पहले खाना बना लिया था। **(had cooked)**
- पुलिस ने चोर को पकड़ लिया था। **(had caught)**
- मैंने जरूरतमंदों की मदद पहले ही कर दी थी। **(had helped)**
- उसने किताब लिखनी शुरू करने से पहले सारी तैयारी कर ली थी। **(had prepared)**
- उन्होंने हमें मुश्किल समय में पढ़ाया था। **(had taught)**
- दुकानदार ने सारे सामान को बेच दिया था। **(had sold)**
- हमने यात्रा के लिए टिकट पहले ही ले लिया था। **(had taken)**
- उसने अपनी साइकिल ठीक कर ली थी। **(had repaired)**

- He **had already taken** the decision.
- I **had decided** to buy a new car.
- He **had already invited** his friends to the party.
- They **had already thought** about it.
- Mother **had cooked** the food before we arrived.
- The police **had caught** the thief.
- I **had already helped** the needy.
- He **had prepared** everything before starting to write the book.
- They **had taught** us during difficult times.
- The shopkeeper **had sold** all the goods.
- We **had already taken** the ticket for the journey.
- He **had repaired** his bicycle.

- उसने अपनी घड़ी ठीक नहीं करवाई थी। **(had not got repaired)**
- उन्होंने बच्चों का ध्यान नहीं रखा था। **(had not taken care of)**
- उसने गाड़ी नहीं चलाई थी, और न ही उसने गाड़ी चलाना सीखा था। **(had not driven, had not learned)**
- हमने पैसे नहीं बचाए थे। **(had not saved)**
- पेड़ बड़े हो चुके थे, लेकिन उन्होंने फल नहीं दिए थे। **(had not borne)**
- उसने फिल्म नहीं देखी थी। **(had not watched)**
- शिक्षक ने छात्रों को निर्देश नहीं दिए थे। **(had not instructed)**
- उसने अच्छे परिणाम की उम्मीद नहीं की थी। **(had not hoped)**
- मैंने उनसे कोई निवेदन नहीं किया था। **(had not made any request)**
- शिक्षक ने उसे कक्षा का मॉनिटर नियुक्त नहीं किया था। **(had not appointed)**
- मैं उनके प्रति कृतज्ञ महसूस नहीं किया था। **(had not felt obliged)**
- उसने मदद करने से इनकार नहीं किया था। **(had not denied helping)**

- He **had not got** his watch **repaired**.
- They **had not taken care of** the children.
- He **had not driven** the car, and he **had not even learned** how to drive.
- We **had not saved** any money.
- The trees **had grown**, but they **had not borne** fruit.
- He **had not watched** the movie.
- The teacher **had not instructed** the students.
- He **had not hoped** for good results.
- I **had not made** any request to them.
- The teacher **had not appointed** him the monitor of the class.
- I **had not felt obliged** to them.
- He **had not denied helping**.

Practice Time 3

- क्या उसने अपना काम खत्म कर लिया था, या वह अभी भी काम कर रहा था? **(Had he finished)**
- क्या तुमने अपनी किताबें पढ़ ली थीं, या तुमने कुछ छोड़ी थीं? (Had you read)
- क्या उसने हमें सही समय पर बुलाया था, या उसने कुछ देर कर दी थी? **(Had he invited)**
- क्या उसने अपनी मेहनत से सफलता हासिल की थी, या उसने किस्मत पर भरोसा किया था? **(Had he achieved)**
- क्या तुमने पहले ही डिनर कर लिया था, या तुम अभी खा रहे थे? **(Had you already had)**
- क्या उन्होंने पार्क में खेला था, या वे घर पर ही थे? **(Had they played)**
- क्या उसने अपनी घड़ी ठीक कर ली थी, या वह उसी हालत में थी? **(Had he repaired)**
- क्या तुमने अपने दोस्तों को पार्टी के लिए बुलाया था, या तुमने किसी को नहीं बताया था? **(Had you invited)**
- क्या वह यात्रा पर जा चुका था, या उसने अभी बुकिंग नहीं की थी? **(Had he already travelled)**
- क्या उसने अपना बैग पैक कर लिया था, या वह सब कुछ छोड़ कर भूल गया था? **(Had he packed)**

- **Had he finished** his work, or was he still working?
- **Had you read** your books, or had you left some?
- **Had he invited** us on time, or had he delayed it?
- **Had he achieved** success through his hard work, or had he relied on luck?
- **Had you already had** dinner, or were you eating now?
- **Had they played** in the park, or were they at home?
- **Had he repaired** his watch, or was it still in the same condition?
- **Had you invited** your friends to the party, or had you told no one?
- **Had he already travelled**, or had he not made the booking yet?
- **Had he packed** his bag, or had he forgotten to pack everything?

यह घर का दृश्य था जो Joy के जागने से पहले का था। सूरज खिड़की के बाहर चमकने लगा था। पक्षियों ने चहचहाना शुरू कर दिया था। माँ ने रसोई में नाश्ता तैयार कर

लिया था। पिता ने अखबार पढ़ लिया था। Jini ने अपनी किताबें जमा ली थीं और वह अपने दोस्तों के साथ बाहर चली गई थी। Furry, हमारा प्यारा पालतूकुत्ता, बगीचे में घूम आया था और अपना सुबह का खाना खत्म करना शुरू कर दिया था। केवल Joy की घड़ी ने कोई अलार्म नहीं दिया था, जिससे उसे पता चलता कि एक नया दिन शुरू हो चुका है।

was, had started, begun, prepared, finished, organized, gone, taken, started finishing, not given, dawned

Speak English - 16

It was the scene of the house before Joy woke up. The sun had started shining outside the window. The birds had begun chirping. Mother had prepared breakfast in the kitchen. Father had finished reading the newspaper. Jini had organized her books and she had gone out with her friends. Furry, the beloved pet dog, had also taken a walk in the garden and started finishing his morning feed. Only Joy's clock had not given any alarm to make Joy know that a new day had dawned.

Write five things that you had done before you went out to Play with your friends.

ज़िंदगी अनिश्चित होती है, और ऐसा ही कल जॉय के साथ हुआ। वह निर्धारित समय से दस मिनट पहले पहुँचा था, यह उम्मीद करते हुए कि छात्र वहाँ होंगे, लेकिन कक्षा खाली थी। उसने परीक्षा के लिए अच्छी तैयारी की थी, लेकिन उसे पता चला कि शिक्षक ने पहले ही परीक्षा को अगले सप्ताह के लिए स्थगित कर दिया था। उसे इस बदलाव के बारे में कोई जानकारी नहीं थी।

happened, had reached, was, prepared, postponed, had no idea

Speak English - 17

Life is unpredictable, and the same happened with Joy yesterday. He had reached ten minutes before the scheduled time, expecting the students to be there, but the classroom was empty. He had prepared thoroughly for the exam, only to discover that the teacher had already postponed it to the following week. He had no idea about the change.

Why was Joy surprised when he reached the classroom?

जब जॉय ने अटारी में एक पुराना डिब्बा देखा, तो उसे बचपन में खोया हुआ खिलौना याद आ गया। वह उसकी पसंदीदा कार थी, जिससे वह हर दिन खेला करता था, जब तक कि वह गायब नहीं हो गई। उसने

तब हर जगह उसे ढूंढा था, लेकिन उसे नहीं मिला। बाद में, उसके माता-पिता ने बताया कि उन्होंने गलती से उसे दे दिया था। जॉय को बहुत दुख हुआ था, लेकिन समय के साथ उसने इसे भुला दिया।

Found, remembered, had lost, had been, had played, went missing, had searched, had not been able to, told, had given, had felt upset, had moved on

Speak English - 18

When Joy found an old box in the attic, he remembered a toy he had lost as a child. It had been his favorite car and he used to play with it every day until it went missing. He had searched everywhere for it back then but had not been able to find it. Later, his parents told him they had given it away by mistake. Joy had felt so upset but over time, he had moved on.

Have you come across any such happening which reminded you of your childhood toy?

जॉय की माँ ने हमेशा उसे सलाह दी थी कि **धीरे-धीरे ही काम पूरा होता है और जल्दबाजी में गलतियाँ होती हैं,** लेकिन वह असाइनमेंट को जल्दी खत्म करने की इतनी

जल्दबाजी में था कि उसने यह सलाह नहीं मानी। वह पूरे दिन उस दस्तावेज़ पर काम कर रहा था, उसमें पूरी जान डालकर। उसने प्रस्तुति को आकर्षक बनाने के लिए दुर्लभ चित्र इकट्ठा किए थे और उसे उम्मीद थी कि यह उसे फाइनल्स में जगह दिलवाएगा। उसने सुरक्षा के तौर पर एक डुप्लिकेट रफ कॉपी भी बनाई थी। लेकिन जब वह फाइल को सहेजने की आखिरी कोशिश कर रहा था, तो उसने गलती से फाइनल वर्शन को डिलीट कर दिया था, रफ कॉपी को नहीं। सोच-समझ कर कदम उठाओ, उसने महसूस किया था, क्योंकि उसने यह सबक कड़ी मेहनत से सीखा था।

had advised, had been, did not listen, had been working, had collected, had hoped, had made, deleted, learned

Speak English - 19

Joy's mother had always advised him that slow and steady wins the race and haste makes waste, but he had been in such a rush to finish the assignment that he didn't listen. He had been working on the document all day, pouring his heart and soul into it. He had collected rare pictures to make the presentation stand out, and he had hoped it would earn him a spot in the finals. He had even made a duplicate rough copy, just in case. But in his final attempt, when he had been in a hurry to save the file, he had accidentally deleted the final version instead of the rough one. Look before you leap, he realized, as he had learnt this lesson the hard way.

Pick proverbs from the passage

जॉय को निमंत्रण बहुत देर से मिला था लेकिन उसने इसका बुरा नहीं माना था। वह जानता था कि कभी-कभी ऐसा होता है। वह उत्साहित था कि पीटर की विदाई पार्टी में वह अपने पुराने दोस्तों से मिलेगा।

जॉय ने जल्दी निकलने की योजना बनाई थी, लेकिन उसने अपनी कार की चाबियाँ खो दी थीं और उन्हें खोजने में एक घंटा लग गया। जब तक वह कार्यक्रम स्थल पर पहुंचे, काफी देर हो चुकी थी। उसे निराशा हुई, उसके सभी दोस्त पहले ही जा चुके थे और हॉल खाली था। वह उनसे मिलने के लिए बहुत उत्सुक था, लेकिन अब वह निराश महसूस कर रहा था। जॉय को एहसास हुआ था कि उसकी देरी के कारण उसे पुराने दोस्तों के साथ फिर से जुड़ने का एक अनमोल अवसर गँवाना पड़ा।

had got, taken ill. planned, misplaced, reached, was, left, had been, felt disheartened, realized

Speak English - 20

Joy had got the invitation very late but he had not taken it ill. He knew sometime it happens. He was excited that he would meet his old friends in Peter's farewell party. Joy had planned to leave early, but he had misplaced his car keys and spent an hour searching for them. By the time he reached the venue, it was already late. To his disappointment, all his friends had already left, and the hall was empty. He had been so eager to catch up with them, but now he felt disheartened. Joy had realized that his delay had cost him a precious opportunity to reconnect with old friends.

Make Sentences
Take it ill, By the time, To his disappointment

यह तब की बात है जब संचार तकनीक उन्नत नहीं थी, और जीवन धीमा और अधिक चुनौतीपूर्ण था। 1980 के दशक में, समाज ने कई समस्याओं का सामना किया था। लोग लंबी दूरी पर जल्दी संवाद करने के लिए संघर्ष किया था। पत्रों को अपने गंतव्य तक पहुंचने में हफ्तों लगे थे। आपातकालीन संदेश अक्सर विलंबित हो गया था, जिससे गलतफहमियां और अवसरों का नुकसान हुआ था। व्यवसायों के लिए दूरस्थ स्थानों में ग्राहकों और साझेदारों से जुड़ना कठिन था। परिवार अपने प्रियजनों से बात करने के साधन न होने के कारण अलग-थलग महसूस किया था।

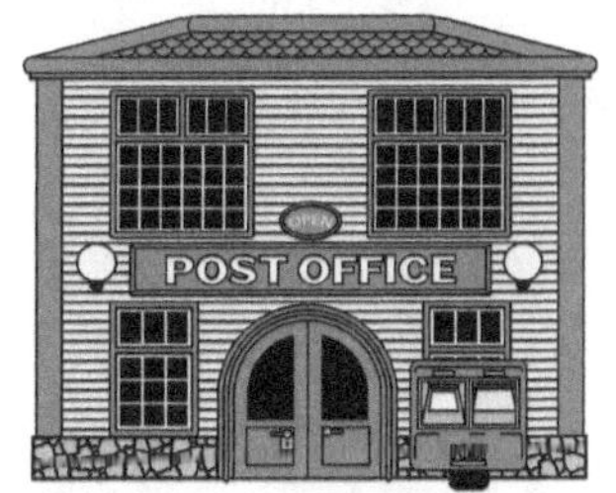

Was asked, trying, making, studying, keeping, submitting, taking, making, balancing

Speak English - 21

It was when telecommunication was not advanced that life had been slower and more challenging. In the 1980s, society had faced many problems. People had struggled to communicate

quickly over long distances. Letters had taken weeks to reach their destinations.

Urgent messages had often been delayed, causing misunderstandings and missed opportunities. Businesses had found it hard to connect with clients and partners in other places. Families

had felt disconnected, as they had no way to talk to loved ones far away.

सचिन तेंदुलकर ने क्रिकेट से संन्यास लेने से पहले कई कीर्तिमान स्थापित कर लिए थे। वह पहले ऐसे क्रिकेटर बन चुके थे जिन्होंने 100 अंतरराष्ट्रीय शतक बनाए थे। वह 2011 में वर्ल्ड कप जीत चुके थे, जो उनका आजीवन सपना था। तब तक उन्होंने टेस्ट और वनडे में सबसे ज्यादा रन बनाने जैसे कई रिकॉर्ड तोड़ दिए थे। सचिन भारत रत्न, भारत का सर्वोच्च नागरिक सम्मान, भी प्राप्त कर चुके थे। इसके अलावा, उन्होंने अपनी निष्ठा और विनम्रता से लाखों लोगों को प्रेरित किया था।

had achieved, retired, become,won,
broken, received, inspired

Sachin Tendulkar had achieved numerous milestones before he retired from cricket. He had become the first cricketer to score 100 international centuries. He had already won the World Cup in 2011, fulfilling his lifelong dream. By then, he had broken countless batting records, including the highest runs in Tests and ODIs. Sachin had also received the Bharat Ratna, India's highest civilian award. Additionally, he had inspired millions with his dedication and humility.

Talk about the achievements your favourite star had made before you knew him/her.

जॉय: हे जैसिका, मैं आखिरकार घर आ गया! ऑफिस में लंबा दिन था। क्या तुमने आज के सारे काम पूरे कर लिए?

जैसिका: ओह, हे जॉय! हां, मैंने ज्यादातर काम तुम्हारे आने से पहले ही पूरे कर लिए थे। मैंने लिविंग रूम साफ कर दिया था और कपड़े भी तह कर दिए थे।

जॉय: यह तो शानदार है! क्या तुमने डिनर बना लिया था, या फिर मैं इसमें मदद करूं?

जैसिका: मैंने डिनर पहले ही बना लिया था। दरअसल, मैंने

तो तुम्हारे कॉल करने और यह बताने से पहले ही टेबल भी लगा दी थी कि तुम रास्ते में हो।

जॉय: कमाल है! लेकिन क्या तुमने पौधों को पानी दिया? वे कल काफी सूखे लग रहे थे।

जैसिका: अरे नहीं! मैंने अभी तक उन्हें पानी नहीं दिया। मैंने सोचा था कि डिनर की तैयारी खत्म करने के बाद पानी दूंगी, लेकिन भूल गई। अभी जाकर पानी देती हूं!

had completed, cleaned, cooked, prepared, set the table, had not watered

Joy: Hey Jassica, I'm finally home! Had a long day at work. Did you manage to get everything done today?

Jassica: Oh, hey Joy! Yes, I had completed most of the chores before you got back. I had cleaned the living room and folded the laundry.

Joy: That's great! Had you cooked dinner, or should I help with that?

Jassica: I had already prepared dinner. In fact, I had even set the table before you called to say you were on your way home.

Joy: Impressive! But had you watered the plants? They looked quite dry yesterday.

Jassica: Oh no! I hadn't watered them yet. I had planned to do it after finishing dinner preparations, but I forgot. I'll do it right away!

सम्राट अशोक, जो अपनी दयालुता के लिए जाने जाते थे, ने आम जनता के कल्याण के लिए अद्भुत पहल की थी। उन्होंने मनुष्यों और पशुओं दोनों के लिए अस्पताल बनवाए थे, जिससे सभी को उचित देखभाल मिल सके। अशोक ने सड़कों और विश्राम गृहों का निर्माण करवाया था ताकि यात्रा आसान हो सके। उन्होंने सड़कों के किनारे छाया और आराम के लिए पेड़ लगवाए थे। इसके अलावा, उन्होंने शांति और अहिंसा के संदेश फैलाए थे, जिससे समाज में सद्भावना बढ़ी।

known, had undertaken, had built, had constructed, had planted, had spread

Speak English - 24

King Ashoka, known for his kindness, had undertaken remarkable initiatives for the welfare of his people.

He had built hospitals for both humans and animals, ensuring proper care for all. Ashoka had constructed roads and rest houses to make travel easier. He had also planted trees along the roads for shade and comfort. Furthermore, he had spread messages of peace and non-violence, promoting harmony among his subjects.

जॉय ने अपने इंटरव्यू के दौरान अंग्रेजी पर कमजोर पकड़ के कारण कई समस्याओं का सामना किया था। वह अपने विचारों को स्पष्ट रूप से व्यक्त करने में  संघर्ष कर रहा था और उसने कुछ महत्वपूर्ण सवालों को गलत समझ लिया था। ज्यादातर समय वह हकलाने या चुप रहने की स्थिति में था। इंटरव्यू लेने वालों ने उसकी कठिनाइयों को देखा और उसे अपनी अंग्रेजी कौशल पर काम करने की सलाह दी। उन्होंने उसकी टेंस की कमजोर जानकारी को नोट किया और उसे **TENSES ARE MY TEACHER** की सभी वॉल्यूम पढ़ने की सिफारिश की, ताकि वह टेंस का अच्छे से अभ्यास कर सके। जॉय ने महसूस किया कि उसमें आत्मविश्वास की कमी थी क्योंकि उसने अंग्रेजी ग्रामर पर काम नहीं किया था।

had faced, struggled, misunderstood, tongue-tied, observed, advised, noticed, realised, lacked, worked on

Speak English - 25

Joy had faced several issues during his interview due to his poor command of English. He had struggled to express his thoughts clearly and had misunderstood a few key questions. Most of the time, he was tongue-tied.

The interviewers had observed his difficulties and advised him to work on improving his English skills.

They had noticed his weak knowledge of tenses and recommended reading all volumes of TENSES ARE MY TEACHER to practice tenses effectively. Joy realized that he lacked confidence because he had not worked on English grammar.

बहादुर सैनिक ने अपनी अंतिम सांस लेने से पहले उल्लेखनीय कार्य किए। उसने बहादुरी से सीमाओं की रक्षा की थी। उसने अपनी टीम का मार्गदर्शन एक प्रकाशस्तंभ की तरह किया था। उसने कई नागरिकों को बचाया था, इससे पहले कि वह अपना बलिदान दे देता। उसने इस कहावत को साबित किया, "संकट के समय ही सच्चा नायक पहचाना जाता है।" उसका बलिदान हमें कैप्टन विक्रम बत्रा जैसे शहीदों की याद दिलाता है, जिन्होंने अंतिम सांस तक लड़ाई लड़ी। सचमुच, उसने कोई कसर नहीं छोड़ी और अपने कर्तव्य का पालन करते हुए शहीद हुआ।

The brave soldier, before breathing his last, accomplished remarkable feats. He  had defended the borders with valor. He had led his team like a guiding light. He had even rescued many civilians before he laid down his life. He lived by the proverb, "A hero is known in the time of trouble," proving his mettle. His sacrifice reminds us of martyrs like Captain Vikram Batra, who had also fought till the last breath. Truly, he left no stone unturned and died with his boots on.

स्वामी विवेकानंद ने अज्ञानता की पकड़ में फंसे समाज में कई झूठी धारणाओं को तोड़ा था। समाज में भेदभाव व्याप्त था, और जाति, रंग और धर्म के नाम पर समाज विभाजित था। उन्होंने असमानता का विरोध किया था और सभी के लिए समानता की वकालत की। उन्होंने इस भ्रांति को चुनौती दी कि महिलाएँ पुरुषों से हीन हैं।उन्होंने उनके अधिकारों के लिए लड़ाई लड़ी और महिलाओं की शिक्षा और सशक्तिकरण के लिए काम किया था। उन्होंने अंधविश्वासों और रीति-रिवाजों को खारिज कर दिया था। उन्होंने इस धारणा को अस्वीकार किया था कि धन किसी व्यक्ति के मूल्य को निर्धारित करता है। उन्होंने आंतरिक चरित्र को महत्व देने पर जोर दिया था। अंत में, उन्होंने इस विश्वास को तोड़ा था कि भारत कमजोर है और इसकी सांस्कृतिक विरासत पर गर्व का संचार किया। उनके प्रयासों ने एक राष्ट्र को जागृत किया था।

had faced, struggled, misunderstood, tongue-tied, observed, advised, noticed, realised, lacked, worked on

Swami Vivekananda had broken several false beliefs gripping society in ignorance. There was discrimination in the society and the society was divided in the name of caste, color and creed. He had opposed inequality and advocated equality for all. He had challenged the misconception that women were inferior. He had fought for their rights and had worked for women education and empowerment. He had dismissed blind rituals. He had rejected the notion that wealth determined a person's worth. He had emphasized on valuing inner character instead. Lastly, he had shattered the

belief that India was weak, instilling pride in its cultural heritage. His efforts had awakened a nation.

डॉ. आर्यन वर्मा ने सफलता का सूत्र खोजने से पहले वर्षों तक अथक परिश्रम किया था। उसने कई प्रयोग किए थे और अनगिनत असफलताओं का सामना किया

था। हालांकि, उसका संकल्प डगमगाया नहीं था। जब उसने अपने निष्कर्ष साझा किए, तब तक उसने विस्तृत रिपोर्ट तैयार कर ली थी। उसके अनुसंधान ने दुनिया भर के युवा वैज्ञानिकों को प्रेरित किया था। लोगों को एहसास हुआ कि उसने तकनीक का भविष्य बदल दिया था। वास्तव में, उसके प्रयासों ने उन नवाचारों की नींव रखी थी जिनका हम आज आनंद लेते हैं। उसका परिश्रम अंततः सफल हो गया था।

had worked, conducted, faced, wavered, prepared, inspired, realized, changed, laid, paid off

Dr. Aryan Verma had worked tirelessly for years before he discovered the breakthrough formula. He had conducted numerous experiments and had faced countless failures. However, his determination had not wavered. By the time he shared his findings, he had already prepared detailed reports. His research had inspired young scientists across the globe. People realized he had changed the future of technology. Indeed, his efforts had laid the foundation for innovations we enjoy today. His hard work had finally paid off.

लाइब्रेरी में प्रवेश करने से पहले शिक्षक ने जॉय और उसके दोस्तों को पाँच महत्वपूर्ण निर्देश दिए थे। उन्होंने उन्हें हर समय चुप्पी बनाए रखने की याद दिलाई थी। उन्होंने पुस्तकों को सावधानीपूर्वक संभालने का निर्देश दिया था। उन्होंने मोबाइल फोन बंद रखने पर जोर दिया था। उन्होंने समय पर पुस्तकें लौटाने के लिए कहा था। अंत में, उन्होंने

लाइब्रेरी के अंदर खाने-पीने के खिलाफ चेतावनी दी थी। ये नियम अनुशासन और सीखने के माहौल के प्रति सम्मान सुनिश्चित करते थे। जॉय और उसके दोस्तों ने शिक्षक से वादा किया था कि वे लाइब्रेरी में शिष्टाचार बनाए रखेंगे।

given, entered, reminded, instructed, emphasized, asked, warned, ensured, promised, maintained

The teacher had given five important instructions to Joy and his friends before they entered the library. She had

reminded them to maintain silence at all times. She had instructed them to handle books with care. She had emphasized keeping mobile phones switched off. She had asked them to return the books on time. Lastly, she had warned them against eating or drinking inside the library. These rules ensured discipline and respect for the learning environment. Joy and his friends had promised the teacher that they would maintain the decorum in the library.

जॉय ने तैरना तब सीखा था जब वह काफी छोटा था। इससे पहले कि वह पूल में कूदे, प्रशिक्षक ने उसे मानसिक और शारीरिक रूप से तैयार किया था। प्रशिक्षक ने जॉय से कहा था कि पानी में शांत और

सहज रहना जरूरी है। उन्होंने उसे अपनी सांसों पर ध्यान केंद्रित करने और उन्हें स्थिर बनाए रखने की सलाह दी थी। उन्होंने जॉय को बताया था

कि ऐंठन से बचने के लिए पूल में प्रवेश करने से पहले हमेशा स्ट्रेचिंग करनी चाहिए। इसके अलावा, प्रशिक्षक ने तैरते समय सिर को शरीर के साथ सीधा रखने के महत्व पर जोर दिया था। अंत में, उन्होंने उसे तैराकी शुरू करने से पहले आत्मविश्वास बढ़ाने के लिए फ्लोटिंग का अभ्यास करने की याद दिलाई थी।

learned, jumped, prepared, advised, informed, emphasized, aligned, reminded

Joy had learned to swim when he was quite young. Before he jumped into the pool, the instructor had prepared him mentally and physically. The instructor had told Joy that it was essential to remain calm and comfortable in the water. He had advised him to focus on his breathing and keep it steady. He had also informed Joy that stretching before entering the pool was necessary to avoid cramps. Additionally, the instructor had emphasized the importance of keeping the head aligned with the body while swimming. Finally, he had reminded Joy to practice floating to build confidence before starting to swim.

- He _____ **(discern)** the error in the report before the meeting began, which helped her provide a better solution.
- By the time I arrived, they _______ **(forfeit)** their chance to compete, which left us disappointed.
- He _____ (contemplate) his decision for days before he finally made it, but he still felt uncertain after ward.
- We _____ **(examine)** all the evidence before the judge made a ruling, which made the trial go smoothly.
- The children _____ **(exhaust)** themselves after hours of playing, so they fell asleep immediately.
- She _____ **(outgrow)** her old hobbies by the time she entered high school, and she began exploring new interests.
- They _____ **(overlook)** the important details in the report, which caused the project to be delayed.
- He _____ **(undermine)** his colleague's authority before anyone realized, so it created unnecessary tension in the office.
- I _____ **(misplace)** my keys earlier, but I _____ **(find)** them just before I left the house, which saved me a lot of time.

- He **had discerned** the error in the report before the meeting began, which helped her provide a better solution.

- By the time I arrived, they **had forfeited** their chance to compete, which left us disappointed.

- He **had contemplated** his decision for days before he finally made it, but he still felt uncertain after ward.

- We **had examined** all the evidence before the judge made a ruling, which made the trial go smoothly.

- The children **had exhausted** themselves after hours of playing, so they fell asleep immediately.

- She **had outgrown** her old hobbies by the time she entered high school, and she began exploring new interests.

- They **had overlooked** the important details in the report, which caused the project to be delayed.

- He **had undermined** his colleague's authority before anyone realized, so it created unnecessary tension in the office.

- I **had misplaced** my keys earlier, but I had found them just before I left the house, which saved me a lot of time.

Practice Answering Questions

1. What had you eaten before you left for work this morning?
2. Had you ever traveled by train before your last vacation?
3. What had you done to prepare before the guests arrived at your house?
4. Had you finished your homework before you went out to play as a child?
5. What had your friend told you before you decided to join the club?
6. Had you ever visited that restaurant before yesterday?
7. What had happened before you realized you had left your wallet at home?
8. Had you tried cooking a new dish before you learned it from a recipe?
9. What had you planned to do before it started raining last weekend?
10. Had you completed all your chores before your parents came home?

Practice Conversation

Joy and Jack's Preparing a Welcome Speech

Joy: Hi Jack, I need your help. I've been asked to give the welcome speech for our class meeting, and I'm so nervous!

Jack: Oh, Joy, that's natural. Everyone feels butterflies in their stomach before speaking for the first time.

Joy: But what if I mess up? What if I forget my words?

Jack: Relax, Joy! Mistakes are a part of learning. Remember, every expert was once a beginner.

Joy: That's true, but I still feel so scared. How can I overcome this?

Jack: Start by practicing in front of a mirror or with a friend. Practice makes perfect, you know.

Joy: Good idea! But what if people don't like my speech?

Jack: Don't worry about that. Just speak from the heart. A sincere speech always touches people.

Joy: Okay, I'll try.

Jack: That's the spirit! Remember, stepping out of your comfort zone is the first step to success.

<u>Joy and Jack: The Best Gifts</u>

Joy: Hi Jack, what's the best gift you've ever received?

Jack: Oh, that's a tough one! But I think it's the bicycle my dad gave me on my 10th birthday. I was over the moon! What about you?

Joy: That sounds amazing! For me, it was a journal my sister gave me. I've always loved writing, and that gift was the cherry on top.

Jack: That's wonderful! Did you fill it up?

Joy: Oh, yes! I wrote poems, stories, even silly doodles. What did you do with your bike?

Jack: I rode it everywhere! It was like having wings. I felt on top of the world every time I pedaled fast.

Joy: Haha, sounds like you really loved it. Did you ever fall off?

Jack: A couple of times! But you know what they say, "Every cloud has a silver lining." Falling taught me to balance better.

Joy: That's a good way to look at it. Gifts like these aren't just things; they're full of memories.

Jack: Exactly! That bike wasn't just a gift; it was my ticket to freedom.

Joy: And my journal wasn't just a book; it was my little world of Ideas. Funny how simple things can mean so much, isn't it?

Jack: Absolutely! They're like treasures that never lose their shine.

A Stroll Down Memory Lane: Finding the Old Library

Joy: You seem a little lost, sir. Can I help you?

Stranger: Oh, thank you! I'm trying to find the old Public Library. I had visited it 30 years ago and hoped to see it again.

Joy: A blast from the past, indeed! Had you spent a lot of time there back then?

Stranger: Absolutely! I had practically lived there during my student days. It was my safe haven.

Joy: I understand. Had you remembered the route, or have things changed too much?

Stranger: I had thought I could find it easily, but the city is a whole new ballgame now!

Joy: True! The library had been relocated to a new building about 15 years ago. Were you aware of that?

Stranger: I had heard something like that, but I wasn't sure. It seems I'm barking up the wrong tree here.

Joy: No worries! Let me point you in the right direction. It's not far from here.

Stranger: Thank you so much! You've really gone the extra mile to help me.

A Bellyful Lesson: Joy's Chat with the Doctor

Joy: "Doctor, I had eaten chips, noodles, and all kinds of junk food before I realized it was a recipe for disaster! Now my stomach feels like it's hosting a storm."

Doctor: "Joy, it seems you had bitten off more than you could chew. This is what happens when you let your eyes be bigger than your stomach."

Joy: "I know, Doctor. By the time the pain hit me, I had already let the cat out of the bag. I had eaten so much, thinking nothing could go wrong."

Doctor: "Well, Joy, you had danced to the devil's tune by indulging in unhealthy snacks. Now, you must pay the piper with some strict dietary rules."

Joy: "I promise, Doctor, I'll never eat like that again. I had taken my health for granted, but this was a wake-up call—a stitch in time saves nine!"

Doctor: "Good to hear, Joy. Remember, prevention is better than cure. Let's get you some medicine to calm the storm in your stomach.

1. Had you **already jumped the gun** (acted too soon) before hearing the full instructions?

2. Had they **burnt the midnight oil** (worked late into the night) to finish the project before the deadline?

3. Had you **let the cat out of the bag** (revealed a secret) before the surprise party began?

4. Had your friends **missed the boat** (lost an opportunity) by ignoring the early registration offer?

5. Had you **taken the bull by the horns** (dealt with a problem directly) before the situation worsened?

6. Had he **kept his nose to the grindstone** (worked hard and continuously) to achieve the promotion?

7. Had she **thrown in the towel** (given up) before even attempting the last round?

8. Had we already **put all our eggs in one basket** (relied on a single plan) before considering other options?

9. Had you **turned a blind eye** (ignored something intentionally) to the warnings before facing the consequences?

10. Had they **been on cloud nine** (felt extremely happy) after receiving the good news?

Describe The Oops Jobs Joy Had Done A few Days Back !

For example :

1. Forgets to take juice in the morning
2. Pours cold water in a glass of hot milk
3. Goes to park instead of going to temple
4. Watches Cartoons instead of attending online class
5. Enters the room with dirty slippers
6. Forgets to water the plants

Describe The Situation and Answer The Given Questions

1. What had the patient not done yesterday?

2. Why had the patient felt unkempt yesterday?

3. Had the patient taken his medicine before today?

4. What tasks has the patient completed today?

5. How does the patient look today compared to yesterday?

1. Why had the young man missed the train?
2. What had the clock above the station indicated before he arrived?
3. Had the train already departed when he reached the platform?
4. What had the young man likely been doing that made him late?
5. How would the situation have been different if he had checked the train schedule earlier?

Describe The Situation and Answer The Given Questions

1. What had the farmer done with the crops before the rain started?
2. Had the farmer repaired the fence before it began to rain?
3. Where had the farmer stacked the hay bales before the storm arrived?
4. Why had the farmer fed the chickens earlier that day?
5. Which seeds had the farmer planted before the sky turned dark?

Make Your Notes

LET'S
GO TO THE NEXT TENSE

FUTURE PERFECT

UNDERSTAND FUTURE PERFECT

Future Perfect Tense की महत्ता

1. भविष्य को समझने में सहायक:

Future Perfect Tense का उपयोग यह बताने के लिए किया जाता है कि कोई कार्य भविष्य में किसी निश्चित समय तक पूरा हो जाएगा। इससे भविष्य के घटनाओं को बेहतर तरीके से समझा जा सकता है और योजना बनाई जा सकती है। उदाहरण:

- I will have finished my homework by tomorrow. (मैं कल तक अपना होमवर्क पूरा कर चुका होऊँगा।)

2. लक्ष्य निर्धारण में मदद:

इस समयकाल का उपयोग किसी कार्य को पूरा करने के लिए लक्ष्य और समय निर्धारित करने में होता है। यह व्यक्ति को अपने कार्यों को प्राथमिकता देने और समय का सही उपयोग करने के लिए प्रेरित करता है। उदाहरण:

- She will have completed the project by the time you arrive. (वह जब तक आप आओगे, परियोजना पूरी कर चुकी होगी।)

3. पूर्वानुमान और भविष्यवाणी:

Future Perfect Tense का उपयोग भविष्य में किसी काम के पूरा होने की संभावना को व्यक्त करने के लिए भी किया जाता है। यह किसी घटना के होने से पहले उसके परिणाम की भविष्यवाणी करता है।

Future Perfect Tense की महत्ता

उदाहरण:

By next year, I will have saved enough money for my trip. (अगले साल तक, मैंने अपनी यात्रा के लिए पर्याप्त पैसे बचा लिए होंगे।)

4. कार्यों का क्रम और महत्व:

Future Perfect Tense यह दिखाता है कि किसी कार्य को पूरा करने की प्राथमिकता और समयसीमा क्या होगी। यह समय का सही इस्तेमाल करने के लिए कार्यों के क्रम को दर्शाता है।

उदाहरण:

- They will have left the office by the time I reach. (वे जब तक मैं पहुँचूँगा, ऑफिस छोड़ चुके होंगे।)

5. आत्मविश्वास और कार्य की योजना:

Future Perfect Tense से व्यक्ति को यह विश्वास मिलता है कि वह किसी कार्य को निर्धारित समय तक पूरा कर सकेगा। यह एक तरह से आत्मविश्वास बढ़ाता है। उदाहरण:

- By the end of this month, we will have achieved our sales target. (इस महीने के अंत तक, हम अपना बिक्री लक्ष्य हासिल कर चुके होंगे।)

UNDERSTAND FUTURE PERFECT

Importance of Future Perfect Tense in English

- Expresses Completion: Shows actions that will be completed before a specific point in the future. Example: "By 5 PM, I will have finished my work."
- Helps in Planning: Useful for discussing future goals or deadlines. Example: "By next month, I will have saved enough money."
- Clarifies Timelines: Makes it clear when something will be finished or expected to happen.
- Enhances Communication: Essential for expressing future expectations and making conversations more precise.
- Common in Professional and Academic Settings: Frequently used to discuss future achievements and milestones.

These sentences use **"will have" + past participle (3rd form)** to indicate actions that will be completed by a specific time in the future.

UNDERSTAND FUTURE PERFECT

In English, both **"will have"** and **"shall have"** are used to form the Future Perfect tense, but they are generally used in slightly different contexts.

1. "Will have" Usage:
- Most common and widely used form for Future Perfect tense.
- Used with all subjects (I, you, he, she, it, we, they) in modern English.

Examples:
- I will have completed the project by tomorrow.
- They will have left by the time you get there.

2. "Shall have" Usage:
- More formal and traditionally used with "I" and "we" in British English.
- "Shall" is often used for future intention or to express something more formal or polite.
- "Will" is now more commonly used even with "I" and "we" in most modern English.

Examples:
- I shall have completed my work by next week. (Formal or traditional)
- We shall have finished our meeting by 3 PM. (Formal tone)

In Modern Usage:
- "Will have" is preferred in almost all situations, even for "I" and "we".
- "Shall have" might still be used in formal writing or in poetry, but "will have" is more common in spoken and casual English.

UNDERSTAND FUTURE PERFECT

Positive Sentences
Example :

1. वह इस समय तक अपना प्रोजेक्ट पूरा कर चुका होगा।
2. हम अगले महीने तक अपना नया घर खरीद चुके होंगे।
3. वह अगले सप्ताह तक अपनी पढ़ाई खत्म कर चुका होगा।

Translations in English:

1. He will have completed his project by this time.
2. We will have bought our new house by next month.
3. He will have finished his studies by next week.

Negative Sentences
Example :

1. वह इस समय तक अपनी यात्रा पूरी नहीं कर चुका होगा।
2. हम अगले महीने तक सभी दस्तावेज़ जमा नहीं कर चुके होंगे।
3. वह अगले सप्ताह तक किसी और नौकरी में काम नहीं कर चुका होगा।

Translations in English:

1. He will not have completed his journey by this time.
2. We will not have submitted all the documents by next month.
3. He will not have started working at another job by next week.

Interrogative Sentences:

Example:
- क्या वह इस समय तक अपनी यात्रा पूरी कर चुका होगा?
- क्या हम अगले महीने तक सभी दस्तावेज़ जमा कर चुके होंगे?
- क्या वह अगले सप्ताह तक किसी और नौकरी में काम कर चुका होगा?

Translations in English:
- Will he have completed his journey by this time?
- Will we have submitted all the documents by next month?
- Will he have started working at another job by next w

"Will have" is used universally and is more common.
"Shall have" is mainly used for I and we in formal contexts or older styles of English.

Practice Time 1

- मैं अगले सप्ताह अपने पड़ोसी के कुत्ते की देखभाल कर चुका होऊँगा। **(look after)**

- वह अपने दोस्त को हवाई अड्डे से लेने आ चुकी होगी। **(pick up)**

- वे अगले महीने तक meeting टाल चुके होंगे। **(put off)**

- वह आज शाम जिम में कसरत कर चुका होगा। **(work out)**

- हम अगले सप्ताह नया कार्यालय स्थापित कर चुके होंगे। **(set up)**

- आप दोपहर 3 बजे तक होटल में चेक-इन कर चुके होंगे। **(check in)**

- बच्चे शनिवार को अपने कमरे साफ कर चुके होंगे। **(clean up)**

- मैं कल अपनी टीम के साथ रिपोर्ट पर चर्चा कर चुका होऊँगा। **(go over)**

- अपनी बैठक के दौरान वह अपने सभी पुराने दोस्तों से मिल चुकी होगी। **(catch up)**

- वे अगले मंगलवार को प्रयोगशाला में प्रयोग कर चुके होंगे। **(carry out)**

- I **will have looked after** my neighbor's dog by next week.
- She **will have picked up** her friend from the airport.
- They **will have put off** the meeting by next month.
- He **will have worked out** at the gym this evening.
- We **will have set up** the new office by next week.
- You **will have checked in** at the hotel by 3 PM.
- The children **will have cleaned up** their room on Saturday.
- I **will have gone over** the report with my team tomorrow.
- She **will have caught up** with all her old friends during the meeting.
- They **will have carried out** experiments in the laboratory next Tuesday.

Practice Time 2

- मैं अगले सप्ताह तक अपने पड़ोसी के कुत्ते को नहीं छोड़ चुका होऊँगा। **(let go)**
- वह अगले महीने तक अपने पुराने सामान को नहीं छोड़ चुकी होगी। **(get rid of)**
- हम अगले साल तक सभी गलतफहमियाँ नहीं सुलझा चुके होंगे। **(sort out)**
- वह कल तक अपने सभी कागजों को नहीं इकट्ठा कर चुका होगा। **(gather up)**
- हम अगले महीने तक परियोजना की योजना नहीं बना चुके होंगे। **(draw up)**
- आप 5 बजे तक अपना सामान नहीं पैक कर चुके होंगे। **(pack up)**
- बच्चे शाम तक अपने खिलौने नहीं सजा चुके होंगे। **(set up)**
- मैं अगले हफ्ते तक अपनी यात्रा की योजना नहीं बना चुका होऊँगा। **(plan out)**
- वह अगले महीने तक अपनी पुरानी आदतों को नहीं छोड़ चुकी होगी। **(give up)**
- वे अगले रविवार तक सभी झगड़े नहीं निपटा चुके होंगे। **(sort out)**

- I **will not have let go** of my neighbor's dog by next week.
- She **will not have gotten rid of** her old belongings by next month.
- We **will not have sorted out** all the misunderstandings by next year.
- He **will not have gathered up** all his papers by tomorrow.
- We **will not have drawn up** the project plan by next month.
- You **will not have packed up** your things by 5 PM.
- The children **will not have set up** their toys by evening.
- I **will not have planned out** my trip by next week.
- She **will not have given up** her old habits by next month.
- They **will not have sorted out** all their arguments by next Sunday.

- क्या राहुल अगले सप्ताह तक अपने पड़ोसी के कुत्ते को देख चुका होगा? **(look after)**
- क्या सिमा अगले महीने तक अपने पुराने सामान को दान कर चुकी होगी? **(give away)**
- क्या आकाश अगले साल तक सारे कागजात जमा कर चुका होगा? **(turn in)**
- क्या रीना कल तक अपनी रिपोर्ट पूरी कर चुकी होगी? **(finish up)**
- क्या हम अगले महीने तक नए उपकरण स्थापित कर चुके होंगे? **(set up)**
- क्या आप 5 बजे तक इस दस्तावेज़ को साइन कर चुके होंगे, अमन? **(sign off)**
- क्या बच्चे अगले सप्ताह तक अपने कमरे की सफाई कर चुके होंगे, नेहा और राहुल? **(clean up)**
- क्या मैं अगले हफ्ते तक अपने परिवार के साथ छुट्टी पर जा चुका होऊँगा, अर्जुन? **(go away)**
- क्या सिमा अगले महीने तक अपनी नई नौकरी शुरू कर चुकी होगी? **(start out)**
- क्या वे अगले मंगलवार तक सभी समस्याओं को हल कर चुके होंगे, विवेक और मोहन? **(sort out)**

- **Will Rahul have looked after** his neighbor's dog by next week?
- **Will Seema have given away** her old belongings by next month?
- **Will Akash have turned in** all the documents by next year?
- **Will Reena have finished up** her report by tomorrow?
- **Will we have set up** the new equipment by next month?
- **Will you have signed off** on the document by 5 PM, Aman?
- **Will the children have cleaned up** their room by next week, Neha and Rahul?
- **Will I have gone away on** vacation with my family by next week, Arjun?
- **Will Seema have started out** her new job by next month?
- **Will they have sorted out** all the issues by next Tuesday, Vivek and Mohan?

इस साल के अंत तक, शहर ने अपने नए मेट्रो प्रोजेक्ट को पूरा कर लिया होगा। मजदूर सभी स्टेशनों का निर्माण पूरा कर चुके होंगे और इंजीनियर सभी ट्रैक की जांच कर चुके होंगे। दिसंबर तक, अधिकारी

नए लाइनों के लिए एक भव्य उद्घाटन की योजना बना चुके होंगे। यात्री मेट्रो का उपयोग करना शुरू कर चुके होंगे और यात्रा करना सभी के लिए कहीं अधिक आसान हो गया होगा। अगले साल की शुरुआत तक, नया सिस्टम यातायात जाम को कम कर चुका होगा और वायु गुणवत्ता में महत्वपूर्ण सुधार हो चुका होगा।

Speak English - 31

By the end of this year, the city will have completed its new metro project. The workers will have finished  constructing all the stations and the engineers will have tested all the tracks. By December, the authorities will have planned a grand inauguration for the new lines. Passengers will have started using the metro and the commute will have become much easier for everyone. By the time the next year begins, the new system will have reduced traffic congestion and the air quality will have improved significantly.

By the end of this year, what will the city have completed, and how will it affect the commute?

अगले साल तक, मैं अपना इंग्लिश कोर्स पूरा कर चुका होऊँगा। मैंने अपनी बोलने की क्षमताओं में सुधार किया होगा और मुझे बहुत आत्मविश्वास मिला होगा।

मैंने अपनी शब्दावली को बढ़ाने के लिए कई किताबें पढ़ी होंगी और कई कार्यशालाओं में भाग लिया होगा। जब तक मैं **IELTS** परीक्षा दूँगा, मैंने सभी आवश्यक कौशल पर अभ्यास कर लिया होगा। मैंने अपने लेखन में सुधार के लिए नई तकनीकें सीखी होंगी और इंग्लिश में कई लोगों से बात की होगी। यह मुझे परीक्षा में उच्च अंक प्राप्त करने में मदद करेगा। साल के अंत तक, मैं अपनी भाषा यात्रा में एक नई ऊँचाई पर पहुँच चुका होऊँगा।

will have completed, improved, gained, read, attended, practiced, learned, spoken, help, reached

Speak English - 32

I will have completed my English course. by the next year. I will have improved my speaking skills, and I will have gained a lot of 

confidence. I will have read several books to enhance my vocabulary and will have attended many workshops. By the time I take the IELTS exam, I will have practiced all the necessary skills. I will have learned new techniques to improve my writing and will have spoken to many people in English. This will help me achieve my goal of scoring high on the exam. By the end of the year, I will have reached a new level in my language journey.

What achievements will the speaker have accomplished in their English learning journey, by next year?

स्कूल ने आज एक निबंध लेखन प्रतियोगिता आयोजित की है। मुझे पता है कि जॉय, जो थोड़ा लापरवाह है, ने कई गलतियाँ की होंगी, जैसे कि खराब तरीके से बनाए गए तर्कों के साथ अपनी कमजोरी को उजागर करना। उसने कई **spelling** की गलतियाँ की होंगी और अपनी खराब लिखावट से स्थिति और भी खराब कर दी होगी। वह समय पर कार्य पूरा नहीं कर पाया होगा और अच्छे अंक पाने का मौका खो दिया होगा। उसकी लापरवाही ने उसे हार का सामना कराया होगा और उसकी सारी मेहनत व्यर्थ चली गई होगी। यह उसके लिए एक कड़वा सच साबित हुआ होगा।

- Letting the cat out of the bag – Revealing a secret.
- Adding fuel to the fire – Making a bad situation worse.
- Missing the boat – Failing to take advantage of an opportunity.
- Gone down the drain – Wasted or lost effort.
- A bitter pill to swallow – A unpleasant truth to accept.

Speak English - 33

The school has organized an essay writing competition today. I know, Joy who is a bit careless, will have made numerous mistakes, letting the cat out of the bag with poorly structured arguments. He will have made many spelling mistakes, adding fuel to the fire with his poor handwriting. He will not have done the task in time, missing the boat to secure a good score. His carelessness will have cost him the game and all his efforts will have gone down the drain. It will have been a bitter pill to swallow for him.

"The only real mistake is the one from which we learn nothing." – Henry Ford

जब जॉय की जन्मदिन की पार्टी शुरू होगी, तब तक बच्चे कई मनोरंजक गतिविधियों में भाग ले चुके होंगे।

उन्होंने म्यूजिकल चेयर, खजाने की खोज और नृत्य प्रतियोगिताओं जैसे खेलों का आनंद लिया होगा।

टॉम ने म्यूजिकल चेयर में उत्कृष्ट फुर्ती दिखाई होगी और सैम ने खजाने की खोज में अपनी सारी बुद्धि का उपयोग किया होगा। कुछ बच्चों ने केक और स्नैक्स खाया होगा, जबकि कुछ ने गुब्बारों से खेला होगा। पार्टी के अंत तक, सभी ने हँसते हुए और यादें बनाते हुए बहुत अच्छा समय बिताया होगा।

Speak English - 34

By the time Joy's birthday party begins, the children will have attended many fun activities. They will have enjoyed games like musical chairs, treasure hunts, and dancing competitions. Tom will have shown excellent swiftness in musical chair and Sam will have used all his wisdom in treasure hunt. Some children will have eaten cake and snacks, while others will have played with balloons. By the end of the party, everyone will have had a great time, laughing and making memories.

> **What activities will the children have completed by the time Joy's birthday party begins?**

जॉय उन सपनों के बारे में अनुमान लगाते हैं जो वह 30 की उम्र तक पूरा कर चुके होंगे। वह नौकरी के क्षेत्र में करियर बनाने का फैसला पहले ही कर चुके हैं, इसलिए वह अपनी मेहनत से करियर में सफलता की सीढ़ियाँ चढ़ चुके होंगे। वह दुनिया के कोने-कोने में घूम चुके होंगे, क्योंकि वह तब तक कम से कम दस देशों की यात्रा करने की इच्छा रखते हैं। उन्होंने मास्टर डिग्री प्राप्त करने के लिए कड़ी मेहनत की होगी और स्पैनिश भाषा में महारत हासिल कर ली होगी, जिससे उन्हें वैश्विक अवसरों के द्वार खुलेंगे। इसके अलावा, उन्होंने अपनी आर्थिक स्थिरता सुनिश्चित करने के लिए पर्याप्त बचत कर ली होगी। इन उपलब्धियों के साथ, जॉय अपने व्यक्तिगत और पेशेवर जीवन में एक खास पहचान बना चुके होंगे।

speculate, achieve, climb, travel, aspire, hit, save, make

Joy speculates about the dreams he will have achieved by the time he turns 30. He will have climbed the corporate ladder, having already decided to pursue a career in the job sector. He

will have traveled the length and breadth of the world, as he aspires to visit at least ten countries by then. He will have hit the books to earn a master's degree and mastered Spanish, opening doors to global opportunities. Additionally, he will have saved enough to feather his nest, ensuring financial stability. With these milestones, Joy will have truly made his mark in both his personal and professional life.

छोटी सी भूरी गौरैया हमारे आस-पास की शोभा और आत्मा है, और उसकी चहचहाहट सभी के लिए खुशी और समृद्धि लाती है। हालांकि, यह स्पष्ट है कि 

आने वाले भविष्य में ये प्राणी हवा में गायब हो जाएंगे। कई पक्षी प्रजातियां अगले पाँच दशकों में वनों की कटाई, प्रदूषण और जलवायु परिवर्तन के कारण विलुप्त हो चुकी होगी। आकाश कब्र के समान शांत हो चुका होगा और प्रकृति के मधुर गीत फीके पड़ चुके होंगे। जंगल अपनी खूबसूरती खो चुके होंगे। और पारिस्थितिक तंत्र असंतुलन में फंस चुके होंगे। उनकी अनुपस्थिति में, पर्यावरण अपनी अनूठी पहचान खो चुका होगा और मानवता उन अद्भुत चीज़ों को फिर से बनाने के लिए व्याकुल होगी, जिन्हें वह कभी संजोती थी।

heart and soul, the writing is on the wall, vanish into thin air, silent as a grave, a feather in its cap, grasping at straws

A little brown sparrow is the heart and soul of our surroundings, and its chirping sounds bring happiness and prosperity to all. However, the writing is on the wall that in the coming future, these creatures will vanish into thin air. Many bird species will have gone extinct in the next five decades due to deforestation, pollution, and climate change. The skies will have become as silent as a grave and the vibrant songs of nature will have faded. Forests will have lost their charm, and ecosystems will have been thrown out of balance. In their absence, the environment will have lost a feather in its cap, leaving humanity grasping at straws to recreate the wonders it once cherished.

"When the last tree is cut down, the last fish eaten, and the last stream poisoned, man will realize that we cannot eat money."

दरबार की कार्यवाही समाप्त होने तक, राजा एक न्यायपूर्ण निर्णय ले चुके होंगे। राजकुमार और उसके मित्र को गरीब किसान

की फसल को मज़े के लिए खराब करने के लिए दंडित किया जा चुका होगा। राजा ने यह आदेश दिया होगा कि वे किसान के खेतों में काम करके और उसकी हानि की भरपाई करके क्षतिपूर्ति करें। प्रजा ने राजा की निष्पक्षता की सराहना की होगी, और राजकुमार ने जिम्मेदारी और दयालुता का महत्वपूर्ण सबक सीख लिया होगा।

will have made, ends, will have been punished, will have decreed, will have praised, will have learned

The king will have made a just decision, by the time the court session ends. The prince and his friend will have been punished for ruining the poor farmer's crops for fun. The king will have decreed that they repay the farmer by working in his fields and compensating for the loss. The kingdom will have praised the king's fairness and the prince will have learned a valuable lesson about responsibility and kindness.

"Justice is the art of restoring what's broken."

गांववालों के चौपाल पर एकत्र होने तक, समझदार बुजुर्ग दो परिवारों के बीच विवाद सुलझा चुके होंगे। उन्होंने दोनों पक्षों की बात सुनी होगी और एक निष्पक्ष समाधान सुझाया होगा। उन्होंने उन्हें यह सलाह दी होगी कि वे ऐसा कुछ न करें, जिससे बाद में उन्हें अपने जीवन में पछताना पड़े। परिवारों ने विवादित जमीन को बराबर बांटने पर सहमति जताई होगी। बुजुर्ग की बुद्धिमानी ने सभी का सम्मान जीत लिया होगा और गांव में शांति बहाल हो चुकी होगी। दिन के अंत तक, गांववाले एकता और सद्भाव का जश्न मना चुके होंगे।

will have resolved, will have listened to, advised, regret, agreed, earned, restored, celebrated

Speak English - 38

By the time the villagers gather in the square, the wise elder will have resolved the dispute between two families. He will have  listened to both sides and proposed a fair solution. He will have advised them not to do anything that make them regret in their life later. The families will have agreed to share the disputed land equally. The elder's wisdom will have earned everyone's respect, and peace will have been restored in the village. By the end of villagers celebrated harmony the day, the will Have unity and together.

व्यस्त बाज़ार में भयानक आग लग गई होगी और जॉय, बिना किसी हिचकिचाहट के, अराजकता में भाग गया होगा। उसने लोगों को आग की लपटों से बचने में मदद की होगी, उन्हें सुरक्षा की ओर मार्गदर्शन किया होगा। कुछ लोग फंस गए होंगे, लेकिन जॉय ने उन्हें निकटतम निकास तक ले जाकर बचा लिया होगा। उनकी त्वरित कार्रवाई से अधिक नुकसान होने से बच गया होगा और बाजार को और अधिक विनाश से बचाया गया होगा । जब तक फायर ब्रिगेड आएगी, जॉय कई लोगों की जान बचा चुका होगा।

will have broken, rushed into, helped, trapped, saved, prevented, saved, arrives, saved

A terrible fire will have broken out in the busy market, and Joy, without hesitation, will have rushed into the chaos. He will have helped people escape the flames, guiding them to safety. Some will have been trapped, but Joy will have saved them by leading them to the nearest exit. His quick actions will have prevented greater loss, and the market will have been saved from further destruction. By the time the fire brigade arrives, Joy will have saved the life of many.

ग्रेस, एक अंधी लड़की, अपनी दृष्टिहीनता के कारण अपने दैनिक जीवन में अनगिनत चुनौतियों का सामना कर चुकी थी। हालांकि, जैसे ही उसे AI-संचालित चश्मे मिले, उसकी दुनिया बदल गई। वह सड़कों पर आत्मविश्वास के साथ आवाज़-निर्देशों के माध्यम से स्वतंत्रता प्राप्त कर चुकी होगी। इन चश्मों ने उसे किताबें और संकेतों को text-to-speech तकनीकी द्वारा पढ़ने में सक्षम बना दिया होगा। वह रियल-टाइम चेहरे की पहचान के कारण दूसरों के साथ बेहतर संबंध अनुभव कर चुकी होगी। सबसे महत्वपूर्ण बात, ग्रेस ने अब अवसरों से भरी हुई एक नई ज़िन्दगी को अपनाया होगा।

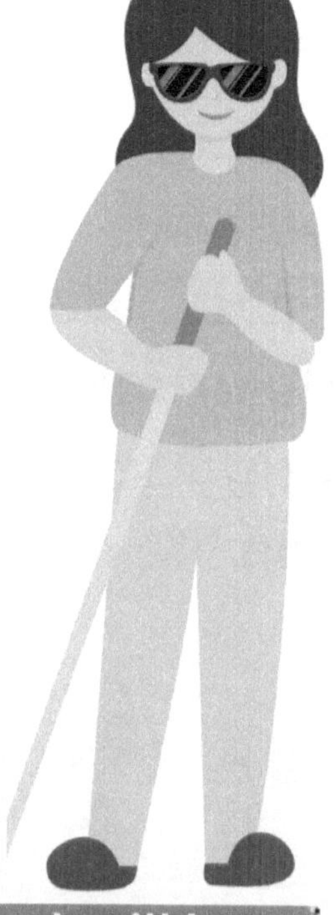

had faced, received, transformed, will have gained, will have enabled, will have experienced, will have embraced

Speak English - 40

Grace, a blind girl, had faced countless challenges in her daily life due to her vision impairment. However, the moment she received her AI-powered glasses, her world transformed. She will have gained newfound independence, navigating the streets confidently with voice-guided directions. The glasses will have enabled her to read books and signs

through text-to-speech technology. She will have experienced greater connection with others, thanks to real-time facial recognition. Most importantly, Grace will have embraced a life full of opportunities.

How will Grace's life have changed after receiving the AI-powered glasses?

Planning a Surprise Birthday Party

अन्ना: जॉय, मैं अपनी बहन के लिए एक सरप्राइज पार्टी प्लान कर रही हूं। मुझे डर है कि क्या मैं शुक्रवार तक सब कुछ संभाल पाऊंगी?

जॉय: कुछ भी मत सोचो। मैं तुम्हारे साथ हूं, और हम इसे मुमकिन बनाएंगे। बस मेरे टाइम प्लान को फॉलो करो, सब कुछ समय पर हो जाएगा।

अन्ना: यह सुनकर राहत मिली! शुक्रवार दोपहर तक मैं घर सजाकर केक भी ऑर्डर कर दूंगी।

जॉय: बढ़िया। आज रात तक, तुमने उसके सभी दोस्तों को इनवाइट कर लिया होगा, है ना?

अन्ना: हां, मैं आज ही उन्हें कॉल कर दूंगी। जब तक वह पहुंचेगी, सब कुछ तैयार हो जाएगा।

जॉय: बिल्कुल! बस प्लान पर टिके रहो, और वह अब तक का सबसे अच्छा सरप्राइज देखेगी!

planning, will have managed, will be arranged, will have decorated, will have invited, arrives, will be ready, will have had

Planning a Surprise Birthday Party

Anna: Joy, I'm planning a surprise party for my sister. I'm scared if I will have managed everything by Friday.

Joy: Don't worry about anything. I'm here to help you make it possible. Just follow my time plan, and everything will be arranged on time.

Anna: That's a relief! By Friday afternoon, I'll have decorated the house and ordered the cake.

Joy: Perfect. By tonight, you'll have invited all her friends too, right?

Anna: Yes, I'll call them today. By the time she arrives, everything will be ready.

Joy: Exactly! Stick to the plan and she'll have had the best surprise ever!

Arranging Accommodation

टीम: जॉय, मुझे मेलबर्न में रहने के लिए अच्छा स्थान ढूंढने की चिंता हो रही है।

जॉय: चिंता मत करो, टीम! मेरे दोस्त जैक ने तुम्हारे आने से पहले सब कुछ सुलझा लिया होगा।

टीम: सच में? वो कैसा स्थान होगा?

जॉय: यह एक उपनगर में स्थित होगा, जहाँ किफायती किराया होगा।

टीम: लेकिन मेरी मुख्य चिंता यह है कि विश्वविद्यालय तक दूरी क्या होगी। मुझे डर है कि रोज़ाना यात्रा में बहुत खर्च हो सकता है।

जॉय: चिंता मत करो, यह विश्वविद्यालय से केवल पैदल दूरी पर होगा।

टीम: यह तो बिल्कुल सही है! कानूनी औपचारिकताओं के बारे में क्या?

जॉय: जैक ने सभी दस्तावेज़ साइन कर लिए होंगे और बिस्तर, किराने जैसी ज़रूरी चीज़ें भी व्यवस्थित कर ली होंगी।

टीम: यह बहुत राहत की बात है, जॉय। मेरी मदद करने के लिए धन्यवाद!

जॉय: कोई बात नहीं, टीम। जब तक तुम मेलबर्न पहुंचोगे, तब तक तुम्हारे पास आराम से बसने के लिए सब कुछ तैयार होगा।

worried, do not worry, will have arranged, will have signed, will have everything ready

Arranging Accommodation

Tim: Joy, I'm worried about finding a good place to stay in Melbourne.

Joy: Don't worry, Tim. My friend Jack will have arranged everything for you before you arrive.

Tim: Really? What kind of place will it be?

Joy: It'll be a suburban setup with pocket-friendly rent.

Tim: But my major concern is the distance to my university. I fear it might cost me a lot for daily travel.

Joy: Don't worry about that—it'll be within walking distance to the university.

Tim: That sounds perfect! What about the legal formalities?

Joy: Jack will have signed all the documents and arranged essentials like beds and groceries.

Tim: That's such a relief, Joy. Thanks for helping me out!

Joy: Anytime, Tim. By the time you reach Melbourne, you'll have everything ready to settle in comfortably.

Role - play this conversation with your speaking partner.

Teacher Unveils Joy's Prank

टीचर: जॉय, मैंने कक्षा में टूटी हुई कुर्सी देखी। मुझे लगता है कि तुम इसके पीछे हो।

जॉय: नहीं, मैं नहीं हूँ! मैं कसम खाता हूँ, मैंने कुछ भी नहीं किया।

टीचर: ह्म्म, मुझे लगता है कि तुमने शरारत सोची होगी, टूटी हुई कुर्सी को स्टोर रूम से लाया होगा, और अपने दोस्तों से चुप रहने को कहा होगा।

जॉय: लेकिन सर, मैं वादा करता हूँ, मुझे इसके बारे में कोई जानकारी नहीं थी।

टीचर: मुझे पूरा यकीन है कि तुमने ऐसा किया। जब कक्षा शुरू हुई, तब तक तुमने इसे अच्छे से सेट कर दिया होगा।

जॉय: नहीं, नहीं! अगर मैंने योजना बनाई होती, तो मैं इसे कहीं बेहतर तरीके से छिपा देता।

टीचर: मैं अब भी यकीन नहीं कर रहा हूँ, जॉय। मुझे पूरा विश्वास है कि तुम दिन के अंत तक शरारत जरूर करोगे!

जॉय: सर, मैं वादा करता हूँ, इस बार मैं निर्दोष हूँ!

noticed, swear, will have brought, would have set, had planned, would have hidden, will have played

Teacher Unveils Joy's Prank

Teacher: Joy, I noticed the broken chair in the classroom. I have a feeling you're behind this.

Joy: No, I'm not! I swear I didn't do anything.

Teacher: Hmm, I think you'll have thought of a prank, brought the broken chair from the storeroom, and asked your friends to stay quiet.

Joy: But, sir, I promise I didn't! I had no idea about this.

Teacher: I'm sure you did. By the time class started, you would have set it up perfectly.

Joy: No, no! If I had planned it, I would have hidden it better!

Teacher: I'm still not convinced, Joy. I'm sure you'll have played a prank by the end of the day!

Joy: Sir, I swear I'm innocent this time!

Role - play this conversation with your speaking partner.

Joy's Mother's Concern For Careless Eating

माँ: जॉय, मुझे यकीन नहीं हो रहा कि तुमने स्कूल ट्रिप के दौरान इतना लापरवाही से खाया। अब देखो, खाना खाने से बीमार हो गए हो!

जॉय: मुझे पता है, मम्मी, मुझे बहुत बुरा लग रहा है। मुझे वो स्ट्रीट फूड नहीं खाना चाहिए था।

माँ: तुम हमेशा खाने के मामले में लापरवाह रहते हो, लेकिन इस बार तो तुमने हद ही कर दी। तुम्हें यह सिखना होगा कि क्या खाना सही है।

जॉय: मैं जानता हूँ, मम्मी। मैं वादा करता हूँ कि मैं फिर से ऐसा गलती नहीं करूंगा।

माँ: तुम्हें तो समझना चाहिए था। अब तक तुम्हें यह सीखना चाहिए था कि ट्रिप्स पर क्या खाना चाहिए और क्या नहीं।

जॉय: मुझे सच में खेद है। मुझे नहीं लगा था कि इससे मुझे इतना बुरा असर होगा।

माँ: तुम्हें अब और जिम्मेदार बनना होगा, जॉय। यह पहली बार नहीं है जब तुमने मेरी सलाह की अनदेखी की है।

जॉय: अब मुझे समझ में आ गया है, मम्मी। अब मैं खाने के मामले में हल्के में नहीं लूंगा।

noticed, swear, will have brought, would have set, had planned, would have hidden, will have played

Joy's Mother's Concern For Careless Eating

Mother: Joy, I can't believe you ate so carelessly on the trip. Look at you now, sick with food poisoning!

Joy: I know, Mom, I feel terrible. I shouldn't have eaten that street food.

Mother: You've always been careless about food, but this time you've gone too far. You'll have to learn to be more careful with what you eat.

Joy: I know, Mom. I promise I won't make the same mistake again.

Mother: You should have known better. By now, you should have learned how to avoid these things during trips.

Joy: I'm really sorry. I didn't think it would affect me like this.

Mother: You'll have to be more responsible, Joy. This isn't the first time you've ignored my advice.

Joy: I understand now, Mom. I won't take food lightly again.

Role - play this conversation with your speaking partner.

Joy and Jessica's Lifelong Journey of Love

जेसिका: जॉय, क्या तुम कभी सोचते हो कि जब हम 70 साल के होंगे, तब हम कैसे होंगे?

जॉय: हमेशा! तब तक, हम एक साथ बहुत सी रोमांचक चीजें करेंगे और एक प्यार भरी जिंदगी जीएंगे।

जेसिका: हाँ! हम साथ में यात्रा करेंगे, बेहतरीन यादें बनाएंगे और हर मुश्किल में एक-दूसरे का साथ देंगे।

जॉय: हमारा प्यार और भी मजबूत होगा। मैं तुम्हारा हाथ पकड़े रहूँगा और तुम्हें अपनी मूर्खतापूर्ण मजाकों से हँसाता रहूँगा।

जेसिका: और हम जिस भी चीज़ को हासिल करेंगे, उस पर गर्व करेंगे, एक खुशहाल और प्यार भरी जिंदगी जीकर।

जॉय: मैं इसका इंतजार नहीं कर सकता, जेसिका। हर पल बहुत खास होगा।

Think, will be, will have traveled, made, supported, grown, holding, making, achieved, can not wait

Joy and Jessica's Lifelong Journey of Love

Jessica: Joy, do you ever think about how we'll be when we're 70?

Joy: All the time! By then, we'll have lived a life full of adventures and love.

Jessica: Yes! We'll have traveled together, made amazing memories and supported each other through everything.

Joy: Our love will only have grown stronger. I'll still be holding your hand, making you laugh with my silly jokes.

Jessica: And we'll be proud of all we've achieved, living a life full of joy and love.

Joy: I can't wait for that, Jessica. Every moment will be worth it.

Role - play this conversation with your speaking partner.

Describe Your Family in Present and How it will have enlarged in Future

ROOM TODAY

ROOM TOMORROW

2025

2035

Describe Your Present Hard Work and Future Success

I WILL STUDY FOR MY EXAMS.
WILL STUDY FOR MY EXAMS.

I WILL BE TAKING MY EXAM NEXT WEEK.

A
I WILL HAVE ARCHEIEVED GREAT RESULTS
REPOCNT
A+

Picture For Practice

1. What will the family do next weekend?
2. What will the family be doing by next week to prepare for the trip?
3. What will the family have done by the time they reach the beach?
4. If you were part of this family, what would you pack for the trip?
5. Do you think the family will enjoy their vacation? Why or why not?

Picture For Practice

1. What is the person planning to do in the first section of the picture?
2. How is the person preparing for the marathon in the second section?
3. What has the person achieved by the end of the journey?
4. How does the picture show the importance of setting goals?
5. Can you describe the progression of the person's fitness journey in your own words?

I have a deep interest in music and am determined to learn how to play the guitar.

Practice Answering The Questions

- By the time you finish school, how many countries will you have visited?
- What will you have accomplished by the end of this year?
- How will you have changed in the next 10 years?
- By the time you get your dream job, how many interviews will you have attended?
- What books will you have read by the time you turn 30?
- Where will you have traveled by the time you retire?
- By this time next week, how many people will you have met?
- How many new skills will you have learned by the time you graduate?
- By the end of this decade, what will you have achieved in your career?
- What will your house look like by the time you're 50?
- By the time you're married, how many weddings will you have attended?
- How will your life have changed by the time you become a parent?

- By the time you're 40, how many family traditions will you have passed down to your children?
- How many lifelong friendships will you have built by the time you turn 50?
- By the time you become a teacher, how many students will you have inspired to pursue their dreams?
- How will the role of leaders in your country have changed by the time you're 60?
- By the time you're 70, how many different neighbors will you have had in your lifetime?
- By the time you're a grandparent, how many of your grandchildren will you have seen grow up?
- By the time you retire, how many leaders in your field will you have mentored?
- How many of your childhood enemies will you have forgiven by the time you're 50?
- By the time you become a parent, how many challenges will you have overcome in your family life?
- By the time you reach 70, how many memorable moments will you have shared with your closest friends?

- By the time you get married, how many traditional rituals will you have followed in your family?
- How do you think society will have changed in the next 20 years?
- By the time you're 50, how many significant cultural traditions will you have participated in?
- How will the education system have improved by the time your children go to school?
- How many environmental reforms will have been introduced in your country by the end of this decade?
- By the time you finish your studies, how many global issues will the education system have addressed?
- How will the healthcare system have evolved by the time you're 60?
- By the time you become a parent, how many changes will have occurred in the way children are educated?
- By the time you reach 70, how many different forms of transport will you have used?
- How many social reforms will have been made in your country by the time you're 40?

Fill in The Blanks

Fill-in-the-blank questions using the present perfect and future perfect tense.

1. She _______ (complete) her homework, and by the time you arrive, she _______ (start) preparing for her exams.
2. The train _______ (leave) the station already, so we _______ (reach) the next stop before noon.
3. I _______ (not see) this movie yet, but by tomorrow evening, I _______ (watch) it with my friends.
4. He _______ (call) you twice today, and he _______ (speak) to your manager before the meeting starts.
5. We _______ (decorate) the house for the party, and by 8 p.m., we _______ (finish) all the arrangements.
6. They _______ (finish) their lunch, and by the time you arrive, they _______ (leave) for the airport.
7. The baby _______ (fall) asleep peacefully, and by the time her parents return, she _______ (wake up).
8. My sister _______ (read) this book already, and she _______ (write) a review of it by next week.
9. The players _______ (practice) hard this season, and by the final match, they _______ (improve) their performance.
10. I _______ (buy) groceries for the week, and by the end of the day, I _______ (cook) dinner for the family.
11. The gardener _______ (water) all the plants, and by the evening, he _______ (trim) the hedges too.
12. Our team _______ (win) two matches so far, and by the end of the tournament, we _______ (secure) the championship.

Answer Sentences

1. She **has completed** her homework, and by the time you arrive, she **will have started** preparing for her exams.
2. The train **has left** the station already, so we **will have reached** the next stop before noon.
3. I **have not seen** this movie yet, but by tomorrow evening, I **will have watched** it with my friends.
4. He has called you twice today, and **he will have spoken** to your manager before the meeting starts.
5. We **have decorated** the house for the party, and by 8 p.m., we **will have finished** all the arrangements.
6. They **have finished** their lunch, and by the time you arrive, they **will have left** for the airport.
7. The baby **has fallen** asleep peacefully, and by the time her parents return, she **will have woken up**.
8. My sister **has read** this book already, and she **will have written** a review of it by next week.
9. The players have practiced hard this season, and by the final match, they **will have improved** their performance.
10. I **have bought** groceries for the week, and by the end of the day, I **will have cooked** dinner for the family.
11. The gardener **has watered** all the plants, and by the evening, he **will have trimmed** the hedges too.
12. Our team **has won** two matches so far, and by the end of the tournament, we **will have secured** the championship.

Fill-in-the-blank questions using the present perfect and future perfect tense.

1. The workers _______ (repair) the roof, and by tomorrow evening, they _______ (complete) the entire building.

2. He _______ (send) the email, and by the time the client responds, he _____ (review) the document.

3. We _______ (explore) several places this month, and by the end of the year, we _______ (visit) all the major tourist attractions.

4. You _______ (submit) your assignment on time, and the teacher _____ (evaluate) it by next week.

5. The chef _______ (prepare) the starters, and by the time the guests arrive, he _______ (finish) cooking the main course.

6. They _______ (organize) two fundraisers already, and by the end of the month, they _______ (raise) enough money for the event.

7. She _______ (learn) three new songs recently, and by her next performance, she _______ (perfect) all of them.

8. I _____ (tidy up) the living room, and by the time you get home, I _______ (clean) the kitchen too.

9. The students _______ (understand) the basics of the topic, and by the final class, they _______ (master) the advanced concepts.

10. He _______ (gain) a lot of experience in this field, and by the end of the year, he _______ (achieve) all his career goals.

1. The workers **have repaired** the roof, and by tomorrow evening, they **will have completed** the entire building.

2. He **has sent** the email, and by the time the client responds, he **will have reviewed** the document.

3. We **have explored** several places this month, and by the end of the year, we **will have visited** all the major tourist attractions.

4. You **have submitted** your assignment on time, and the teacher **will have evaluated** it by next week.

5. The chef **has prepared** the starters, and by the time the guests arrive, he **will have finished** cooking the main course.

6. They **have organized** two fundraisers already, and by the end of the month, they **will have raised** enough money for the event.

7. She **has learned** three new songs recently, and by her next performance, she **will have perfected** all of them.

8. I **have tidied up** the living room, and by the time you get home, I **will have cleaned** the kitchen too.

9. The students have understood the basics of the topic, and by the final class, they **will have mastered** the advanced concepts.

10. He **has gained** a lot of experience in this field, and by the end of the year, he **will have achieved** all his career goals.

1. **"Life in 2050: Predicting the Future"**
   - Imagine how technology, education, transportation, and daily life will have evolved by 2050. Encourage sentences like:
     - "By 2050, self-driving cars will have replaced traditional vehicles."
     - "People will live in smart homes with AI assistants."
2. **"My Future Dream Vacation"**
   - Describe a vacation they are planning or imagining. Example sentences:
     - "I will visit Paris and take a tour of the Eiffel Tower."
     - "By the end of the trip, I will have explored all the major landmarks."
3. **"Achievements of the Next Decade"**
   - Students discuss their personal goals and ambitions for the next ten years. Example sentences:
     - "I will graduate from college and start my dream job."
     - "By 2034, I will have published my first book."
4. **"The Future of Our Planet"**
   - Predict environmental changes and technological innovations that will shape the Earth. Example sentences:
     - "We will develop sustainable energy solutions."
     - "By 2050, we will have significantly reduced plastic waste."

5. **"Technological Innovations in the Next 20 Years"**
   - Discuss new inventions or advancements in technology. Example sentences:
     - "In the next 20 years, robots will help with everyday tasks."
     - "By 2044, we will have developed fully functional flying cars."

6. **"How I Will Improve My Health in the Future"**
   - Talk about personal goals for health and fitness. Example sentences:
     - "I will start exercising regularly and eat a balanced diet."
     - "By next year, I will have reached my fitness goals and feel healthier."

7. **"The Future of Education"**
   - Predict changes in how people will learn in the coming years. Example sentences:
     - "Schools will offer more virtual learning options."
     - "By 2030, we will have integrated AI into all classrooms to personalize learning."

8. **"Future Careers: What Jobs Will Be in Demand?"**
   - Explore the types of jobs that will exist in the future. Example sentences:
     - "In the future, people will work in careers related to artificial intelligence and space exploration."
     - "By 2040, we will have created jobs that don't even exist today."

Practice with Verbs

VERBS	VERBS SYNONYMS
1. WILL HAVE HELPED	WILL HAVE ASSISTED
2. WILL HAVE THOUGHT	WILL HAVE SPECULATED
3. WILL HAVE GONE	WILL HAVE DEPARTED
4. WILL HAVE MADE	WILL HAVE CREATED
5. WILL HAVE SEEN	WILL HAVE WITNESSED
6. WILL HAVE CHOSEN	WILL HAVE SELECTED
7. WILL HAVE FINISHED	WILL HAVE COMPLETED
8. WILL HAVE LEARNED	WILL HAVE DISCOVERED
9. WILL HAVE DONE	WILL HAVE ACCOMPLISHED
10. WILL HAVE WRITTEN	WILL HAVE COMPOSED
11. WILL HAVE SPOKEN	WILL HAVE ADDRESSED
12. WILL HAVE MET	WILL HAVE ENCOUNTERED
13. WILL HAVE BUILT	WILL HAVE CONSTRUCTED
14. WILL HAVE TRIED	WILL HAVE ATTEMPTED
15. WILL HAVE RECEIVED	WILL HAVE OBTAINED

Practice with Verbs

VERB	SYNONYM
WILL HAVE ASSISTED	WILL HAVE HELPED
WILL HAVE COMPOSED	WILL HAVE CREATED
WILL HAVE ENCOUNTERED	WILL HAVE MET
WILL HAVE PERCEIVED	WILL HAVE NOTICED
WILL HAVE EXPLAINED	WILL HAVE DESCRIBED
WILL HAVE CONSTRUCTED	WILL HAVE BUILT
WILL HAVE REJECTED	WILL HAVE DECLINED
WILL HAVE ACCEPTED	WILL HAVE AGREED
WILL HAVE CONQUERED	WILL HAVE DEFEATED
WILL HAVE PURCHASED	WILL HAVE BOUGHT
WILL HAVE DECLARED	WILL HAVE ANNOUNCED
WILL HAVE OBLIGED	WILL HAVE REQUIRED
WILL HAVE DISCOVERED	WILL HAVE FOUND
WILL HAVE EXPECTED	WILL HAVE ANTICIPATED
WILL HAVE FORGOTTEN	WILL HAVE OVERLOOKED
WILL HAVE MAINTAINED	WILL HAVE PRESERVED

Practice with Verbs

Verb	Synonym
Will have praised	Will have admired
Will have criticized	Will have condemned
Will have achieved	Will have attained
Will have clarified	Will have explained
Will have negotiated	Will have bargained
Will have procrastinated	Will have delayed
Will have analyzed	Will have examined
Will have transformed	Will have altered
Will have initiated	Will have started
Will have implemented	Will have executed
Will have innovated	Will have created
Will have endured	Will have tolerated
Will have justified	Will have defended
Will have rectified	Will have corrected
Will have dictated	Will have commanded
Will have ascertained	Will have determined

Practice with Verbs

VERBS	VERBS SYNONYMS
1. WILL HAVE EXAMINED	WILL HAVE INSPECTED
2. WILL HAVE EARNED	WILL HAVE ACQUIRED
3. WILL HAVE PREDICTED	WILL HAVE FORECASTED
4. WILL HAVE SOLVED	WILL HAVE RESOLVED
5. WILL HAVE INFLUENCED	WILL HAVE IMPACTED
6. WILL HAVE PROVEN	WILL HAVE DEMONSTRATED
7. WILL HAVE GENERATED	WILL HAVE PRODUCED
8. WILL HAVE REVISED	WILL HAVE AMENDED
9. WILL HAVE CONSOLIDATED	WILL HAVE STRENGTHENED
10. WILL HAVE CLARIFIED	WILL HAVE EXPLAINED
11. WILL HAVE DEVELOPED	WILL HAVE EVOLVED
12. WILL HAVE INTEGRATED	WILL HAVE INCORPORATED
13. WILL HAVE SIMULATED	WILL HAVE MODELED
14. WILL HAVE TRANSLATED	WILL HAVE INTERPRETED
15. WILL HAVE REACTED	WILL HAVE RESPONDED

TENSE CHART

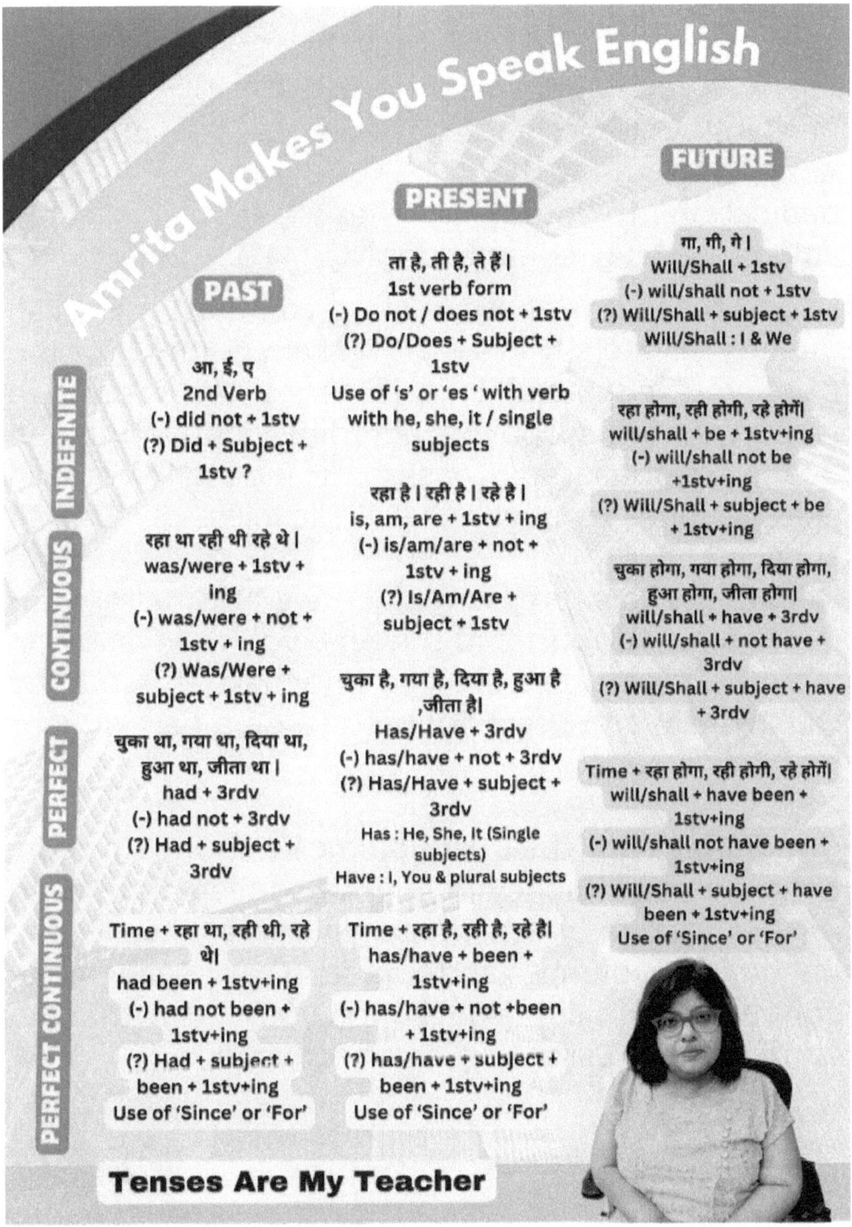
Amrita Makes You Speak English
PAST
PRESENT
FUTURE
INDEFINITE
CONTINUOUS
PERFECT
PERFECT CONTINUOUS
आ, ई, ए
2nd Verb
(-) did not + 1stv
(?) Did + Subject + 1stv ?
ता है, ती है, ते हैं |
1st verb form
(-) Do not / does not + 1stv
(?) Do/Does + Subject + 1stv
Use of 's' or 'es ' with verb with he, she, it / single subjects
गा, गी, गे |
Will/Shall + 1stv
(-) will/shall not + 1stv
(?) Will/Shall + subject + 1stv
Will/Shall : I & We
रहा था रही थी रहे थे |
was/were + 1stv + ing
(-) was/were + not + 1stv + ing
(?) Was/Were + subject + 1stv + ing
रहा है | रही है | रहे है |
is, am, are + 1stv + ing
(-) is/am/are + not + 1stv + ing
(?) Is/Am/Are + subject + 1stv
रहा होगा, रही होगी, रहे होगें|
will/shall + be + 1stv+ing
(-) will/shall not be +1stv+ing
(?) Will/Shall + subject + be + 1stv+ing
चुका था, गया था, दिया था, हुआ था, जीता था |
had + 3rdv
(-) had not + 3rdv
(?) Had + subject + 3rdv
चुका है, गया है, दिया है, हुआ है ,जीता है|
Has/Have + 3rdv
(-) has/have + not + 3rdv
(?) Has/Have + subject + 3rdv
Has : He, She, It (Single subjects)
Have : I, You & plural subjects
चुका होगा, गया होगा, दिया होगा, हुआ होगा, जीता होगा|
will/shall + have + 3rdv
(-) will/shall + not have + 3rdv
(?) Will/Shall + subject + have + 3rdv
Time + रहा था, रही थी, रहे थे|
had been + 1stv+ing
(-) had not been + 1stv+ing
(?) Had + subject + been + 1stv+ing
Use of 'Since' or 'For'
Time + रहा है, रही है, रहे है|
has/have + been + 1stv+ing
(-) has/have + not +been + 1stv+ing
(?) has/have + subject + been + 1stv+ing
Use of 'Since' or 'For'
Time + रहा होगा, रही होगी, रहे होगें|
will/shall + have been + 1stv+ing
(-) will/shall not have been + 1stv+ing
(?) Will/Shall + subject + have been + 1stv+ing
Use of 'Since' or 'For'
Tenses Are My Teacher

Message Of Thanks

Dear Reader,

Thank you immensely for finishing Volume 5 of "Tenses Are My Teacher." Your dedication to studying these volumes is truly commendable.

I hope these books are helping you master English fluently, especially in speaking. I am grateful for the trust you've placed in this series. Your positive response to the book is incredibly motivating and deeply appreciated. Tenses are indeed pivotal in guiding one through the intricacies of English speech.

I would like to express my sincere gratitude for your continuous support and the time you've invested in learning. It's readers like you who make this journey worthwhile, and I feel honored to be a part of your learning experience.

Continuing with the next volumes will undoubtedly enhance your fluency in English conversation even further. I eagerly anticipate your presence in the upcoming volume and hope that each page continues to contribute to your growth and confidence in using English effectively!

Warm regards,
AMRITASHAAN

ALL VOLUMES OF TENSES ARE MY TEACHER

Make Your Notes

Make Your Notes